Proper Education Group

# 4 Practice Tests for the Michigan Real Estate Exam

"The secret to getting ahead is getting started."
Mark Twain

# Table of Contents

# Introduction

## 1.1 Requirements

On the day of the test, you must bring the following:

1. **TWO** forms of valid and non-expired government-issued ID with a valid signature. One must be government issued and include a photo. Examples include:
   a. Driver's license
   b. State issued identification (ex. non-driver ID)
   c. United States Passport
   d. Credit card
2. A second ID that contains your signature and legal name
3. A basic non-scientific calculator

You are not required to bring a calculator, but you are **highly encouraged to do so** as there will be simple mathematical questions that require multiplication and division. Do not rely on the one on your phone because **phones will not be allowed**.

## 1.2 About the Exam

The test is 3 hours long and composed of two sections.

The national portion is composed of 80 multiple choice questions and the state portion is composed of 35 multiple choice questions.

You must answer at least 70% of all questions to pass.

The exam is administered through a computer.

## 1.3 How to Apply

To apply for the exam, visit the website below and submit the required the forms:

https://www.michigan.gov/lara/0,4601,7-154-89334_72600_72602_72731_72871-360474--,00.html

All of the official documentation pertaining payments, documents, and forms can be found there.

## 1.4 Exam Results

Your score will be given to you immediately after finishing the exam.

# Practice Test 1

Directions:

1.    You have a 3-hour time limit to complete the whole exam.

2.    To pass, you must answer at least 70% of all questions correctly.

3.    Some questions will require mathematics. You may use a calculator.

4.    **Phones and pagers are not allowed. Having either will result in automatic dismissal from the exam and nullification of exam scores.**

Tips:

- Answer all questions even if you are unsure.
- Mark any questions you are stuck on and revisit them after you are done. The exam is timed so make sure you finish as many questions as you can.
- After reading the question, try answering it in your head first to avoid getting confused by the choices.
- Read the entire question before looking at the answers.
- Use the process of elimination to filter out choices that don't seem correct to increase your chances of selecting the correct answer.
- Be aware of important keywords like **not, sometimes, always,** and **never**. These words completely alter the ask of the question so it's important to keep track of them.

**PLEASE READ THESE INSTRUCTIONS CAREFULLY.**

Name: _____          Date: _____

## NATIONAL PORTION

| 1. | Ⓐ Ⓑ Ⓒ Ⓓ | 31. | Ⓐ Ⓑ Ⓒ Ⓓ | 61. | Ⓐ Ⓑ Ⓒ Ⓓ |
|---|---|---|---|---|---|
| 2. | Ⓐ Ⓑ Ⓒ Ⓓ | 32. | Ⓐ Ⓑ Ⓒ Ⓓ | 62. | Ⓐ Ⓑ Ⓒ Ⓓ |
| 3. | Ⓐ Ⓑ Ⓒ Ⓓ | 33. | Ⓐ Ⓑ Ⓒ Ⓓ | 63. | Ⓐ Ⓑ Ⓒ Ⓓ |
| 4. | Ⓐ Ⓑ Ⓒ Ⓓ | 34. | Ⓐ Ⓑ Ⓒ Ⓓ | 64. | Ⓐ Ⓑ Ⓒ Ⓓ |
| 5. | Ⓐ Ⓑ Ⓒ Ⓓ | 35. | Ⓐ Ⓑ Ⓒ Ⓓ | 65. | Ⓐ Ⓑ Ⓒ Ⓓ |
| 6. | Ⓐ Ⓑ Ⓒ Ⓓ | 36. | Ⓐ Ⓑ Ⓒ Ⓓ | 66. | Ⓐ Ⓑ Ⓒ Ⓓ |
| 7. | Ⓐ Ⓑ Ⓒ Ⓓ | 37. | Ⓐ Ⓑ Ⓒ Ⓓ | 67. | Ⓐ Ⓑ Ⓒ Ⓓ |
| 8. | Ⓐ Ⓑ Ⓒ Ⓓ | 38. | Ⓐ Ⓑ Ⓒ Ⓓ | 68. | Ⓐ Ⓑ Ⓒ Ⓓ |
| 9. | Ⓐ Ⓑ Ⓒ Ⓓ | 39. | Ⓐ Ⓑ Ⓒ Ⓓ | 69. | Ⓐ Ⓑ Ⓒ Ⓓ |
| 10. | Ⓐ Ⓑ Ⓒ Ⓓ | 40. | Ⓐ Ⓑ Ⓒ Ⓓ | 70. | Ⓐ Ⓑ Ⓒ Ⓓ |
| 11. | Ⓐ Ⓑ Ⓒ Ⓓ | 41. | Ⓐ Ⓑ Ⓒ Ⓓ | 71. | Ⓐ Ⓑ Ⓒ Ⓓ |
| 12. | Ⓐ Ⓑ Ⓒ Ⓓ | 42. | Ⓐ Ⓑ Ⓒ Ⓓ | 72. | Ⓐ Ⓑ Ⓒ Ⓓ |
| 13. | Ⓐ Ⓑ Ⓒ Ⓓ | 43. | Ⓐ Ⓑ Ⓒ Ⓓ | 73. | Ⓐ Ⓑ Ⓒ Ⓓ |
| 14. | Ⓐ Ⓑ Ⓒ Ⓓ | 44. | Ⓐ Ⓑ Ⓒ Ⓓ | 74. | Ⓐ Ⓑ Ⓒ Ⓓ |
| 15. | Ⓐ Ⓑ Ⓒ Ⓓ | 45. | Ⓐ Ⓑ Ⓒ Ⓓ | 75. | Ⓐ Ⓑ Ⓒ Ⓓ |
| 16. | Ⓐ Ⓑ Ⓒ Ⓓ | 46. | Ⓐ Ⓑ Ⓒ Ⓓ | 76. | Ⓐ Ⓑ Ⓒ Ⓓ |
| 17 | Ⓐ Ⓑ Ⓒ Ⓓ | 47. | Ⓐ Ⓑ Ⓒ Ⓓ | 77. | Ⓐ Ⓑ Ⓒ Ⓓ |
| 18. | Ⓐ Ⓑ Ⓒ Ⓓ | 48. | Ⓐ Ⓑ Ⓒ Ⓓ | 78. | Ⓐ Ⓑ Ⓒ Ⓓ |
| 19. | Ⓐ Ⓑ Ⓒ Ⓓ | 49. | Ⓐ Ⓑ Ⓒ Ⓓ | 79. | Ⓐ Ⓑ Ⓒ Ⓓ |
| 20. | Ⓐ Ⓑ Ⓒ Ⓓ | 50. | Ⓐ Ⓑ Ⓒ Ⓓ | 80. | Ⓐ Ⓑ Ⓒ Ⓓ |
| 21. | Ⓐ Ⓑ Ⓒ Ⓓ | 51. | Ⓐ Ⓑ Ⓒ Ⓓ | | |
| 22. | Ⓐ Ⓑ Ⓒ Ⓓ | 52. | Ⓐ Ⓑ Ⓒ Ⓓ | | |
| 23. | Ⓐ Ⓑ Ⓒ Ⓓ | 53. | Ⓐ Ⓑ Ⓒ Ⓓ | | |
| 24. | Ⓐ Ⓑ Ⓒ Ⓓ | 54. | Ⓐ Ⓑ Ⓒ Ⓓ | | |
| 25. | Ⓐ Ⓑ Ⓒ Ⓓ | 55. | Ⓐ Ⓑ Ⓒ Ⓓ | | |
| 26. | Ⓐ Ⓑ Ⓒ Ⓓ | 56. | Ⓐ Ⓑ Ⓒ Ⓓ | | |
| 27. | Ⓐ Ⓑ Ⓒ Ⓓ | 57. | Ⓐ Ⓑ Ⓒ Ⓓ | | |
| 28. | Ⓐ Ⓑ Ⓒ Ⓓ | 58. | Ⓐ Ⓑ Ⓒ Ⓓ | | |
| 29. | Ⓐ Ⓑ Ⓒ Ⓓ | 59. | Ⓐ Ⓑ Ⓒ Ⓓ | | |
| 30. | Ⓐ Ⓑ Ⓒ Ⓓ | 60. | Ⓐ Ⓑ Ⓒ Ⓓ | | |

Practice Tes

Name: _____          Date: _____

STATE PORTION

| 1. | Ⓐ Ⓑ Ⓒ Ⓓ | 31. | Ⓐ Ⓑ Ⓒ Ⓓ |
|----|----------|-----|----------|
| 2. | Ⓐ Ⓑ Ⓒ Ⓓ | 32. | Ⓐ Ⓑ Ⓒ Ⓓ |
| 3. | Ⓐ Ⓑ Ⓒ Ⓓ | 33. | Ⓐ Ⓑ Ⓒ Ⓓ |
| 4. | Ⓐ Ⓑ Ⓒ Ⓓ | 34. | Ⓐ Ⓑ Ⓒ Ⓓ |
| 5. | Ⓐ Ⓑ Ⓒ Ⓓ | 35. | Ⓐ Ⓑ Ⓒ Ⓓ |
| 6. | Ⓐ Ⓑ Ⓒ Ⓓ | | |
| 7. | Ⓐ Ⓑ Ⓒ Ⓓ | | |
| 8. | Ⓐ Ⓑ Ⓒ Ⓓ | | |
| 9. | Ⓐ Ⓑ Ⓒ Ⓓ | | |
| 10. | Ⓐ Ⓑ Ⓒ Ⓓ | | |
| 11. | Ⓐ Ⓑ Ⓒ Ⓓ | | |
| 12. | Ⓐ Ⓑ Ⓒ Ⓓ | | |
| 13. | Ⓐ Ⓑ Ⓒ Ⓓ | | |
| 14. | Ⓐ Ⓑ Ⓒ Ⓓ | | |
| 15. | Ⓐ Ⓑ Ⓒ Ⓓ | | |
| 16. | Ⓐ Ⓑ Ⓒ Ⓓ | | |
| 17 | Ⓐ Ⓑ Ⓒ Ⓓ | | |
| 18. | Ⓐ Ⓑ Ⓒ Ⓓ | | |
| 19. | Ⓐ Ⓑ Ⓒ Ⓓ | | |
| 20. | Ⓐ Ⓑ Ⓒ Ⓓ | | |
| 21. | Ⓐ Ⓑ Ⓒ Ⓓ | | |
| 22. | Ⓐ Ⓑ Ⓒ Ⓓ | | |
| 23. | Ⓐ Ⓑ Ⓒ Ⓓ | | |
| 24. | Ⓐ Ⓑ Ⓒ Ⓓ | | |
| 25. | Ⓐ Ⓑ Ⓒ Ⓓ | | |
| 26. | Ⓐ Ⓑ Ⓒ Ⓓ | | |
| 27. | Ⓐ Ⓑ Ⓒ Ⓓ | | |
| 28. | Ⓐ Ⓑ Ⓒ Ⓓ | | |
| 29. | Ⓐ Ⓑ Ⓒ Ⓓ | | |
| 30. | Ⓐ Ⓑ Ⓒ Ⓓ | | |

## National Portion

1. When applying for a loan, what is a **fixed rate**?

   A. A loan that has a predetermined repayment interest rate
   B. A loan that has an interest rate that varies over time
   C. A loan that accrues no interest
   D. A loan that pays off the interest before the principal

2. What act prohibits discrimination based on race or color?

   A. Fair Housing Act
   B. Civil Rights Act of 1866
   C. Civil Right Act of 1964
   D. Civil Rights Act Amendment of 1974

3. What is the financial document that contains a written promise to fulfill a certain payment?

   A. Invoice
   B. Promissory note
   C. Pro forma statement
   D. IOU

4. What is the term used to describe the act of replacing an existing mortgage with another?

   A. Refinancing
   B. Defaulting
   C. Foreclosure
   D. Reinvesting

5. Which is **not** an appurtenant right?

   A. Furnace
   B. Swimming pool
   C. Air conditioning
   D. All of the above

6. What is the name given to the banking option that allows a customer to deposit a specified amount for a predetermined period of time?

   A. Certificate of occupation
   B. Certificate of deposit
   C. Investment clause
   D. Mortgage

7. If a seller nets $225,000 after paying a 10% fee, what was the total he received?

   A. $202,500
   B. $224,990
   C. $250,000
   D. None of the above

8. What is the name given to the rate earned for borrowing or an investment per year?

   A. Rate lock
   B. Fixed rate
   C. Floating rate
   D. Annual percentage rate

9. Other than buying a home using traditional channels, what other methods can a prospective owner use to buy a home?

   A. Public auctions
   B. Tender
   C. Lease
   D. Escalation clause

10. What is the reviewing of a borrower's credit worthiness prior to loan approval?

    A. Buydown
    B. Pre-qualification
    C. Credit score
    D. Under qualification

11. What is the document that is used to transfer legal rights to act in the interest of a person?

    A. Disclosure form
    B. Power of attorney
    C. Pro forma statement
    D. Deed

12. What type of listing only guarantees commission for a sale within a specified period?

    A. Exclusive listing
    B. Net listing
    C. Single agency listing
    D. Multi agency listing

13. What type of brokerage mandates that the broker acts in the best interest of the buyer?

    A. Single agency
    B. Dual agency
    C. Multi agency
    D. Full service

14. What is the name of a transaction where both the buyer and seller are seeking the best deal?

    A. Real estate transaction
    B. Credit transaction
    C. Arms-length transaction
    D. Debited transaction

15. What is the name given to modification of billing calculation dates?

    A. Modified date
    B. Closing date
    C. Opening date
    D. Adjustment date

16. What is the name of the mortgage that is transferred by the seller to the buyer?

    A. Assumable mortgage
    B. Adjusted rate mortgage
    C. Fixed rate mortgage
    D. Floating mortgage

**17.** What is the contract that secures a future transaction?

  A. Deed
  B. Call option
  C. Title
  D. None of the above

**18.** What does an exclusive listing contract need to be considered valid?

  A. A net listing
  B. A commission rate of at least 6%
  C. A specified expiration date
  D. The signature of the grantee

**19.** What is it when another state recognizes your real estate license?

  A. Transfer
  B. Limited basis policy
  C. Reciprocity
  D. None of the above

**20.** Which of the following is **not** a fiduciary duty?

  A. Accounting
  B. Confidentiality
  C. Obedience
  D. Privacy

**21.** What are contingencies as used in real estate?

  A. Conditions that must be met by both the buyer and the seller before closing
  B. Conditions set by the government on buying a home
  C. Conditions set by the bank in order to approve a loan for a mortgage
  D. Conditions that must be met to avoid judicial foreclosure

**22.** Who is a co-borrower?

  A. Any individual whose name appears on the loan document
  B. Someone that borrows money at the same time with you
  C. The mortgage broker that originates the loan for you
  D. An individual that guarantees your loan

**23.** What is the name given to a loan taken out to finance construction?

  A. Mortgage
  B. Construction loan
  C. Business loan
  D. Personal loan

**24.** What is the name given to the inspection done by the buyer before closing?

  A. Final inspection
  B. Advertorial
  C. Housing ratio
  D. Final walkthrough

25. What is the name given to a mortgage whose interest rate does **not** change throughout the payment period?

    A. Adjustable mortgage rate
    B. Floating rate
    C. Fixed mortgage rate
    D. Bridge loan

26. What is defined as the percentage owned by the buyer after making a down payment?

    A. Housing ratio
    B. Debt to income ratio
    C. Loan to value ratio
    D. Floating rate

27. What is the cash on cash return of a $60,000 investment that generates $1,000 in monthly cash flow?

    A. 1.67%
    B. 2%
    C. 20%
    D. None of the above

28. What is the term used to refer to the responsibility one individual has for the acts of another?

    A. Vicarious liability
    B. Fixed liability
    C. Current liability
    D. Contingent

29. What is the name given to a form used to explain the role of an agent in a real estate transaction?

    A. Purchase agreement
    B. Accountability
    C. Assignment contract
    D. Agency disclosure statement

30. A number of brokers agreed on a set standard commission. What antitrust law are they guilty of violating?

    A. Commingling
    B. Price fixing
    C. Steering
    D. Discussing

31. Which government agency is responsible for determining the status of an independent contractor?

    A. Federal government
    B. Bank
    C. Department of State
    D. IRS

32. What is the nature of the title issued in condo ownership?

    A. Freehold
    B. Regular
    C. Deed
    D. Clear title

**33.** Mr. and Mrs. Johnson made a $350,000 profit on the sale of their primary home. How much do they owe in capital gains tax?

A. $0
B. $3,500
C. $50,000
D. Half of the amount earned

**34.** What is the status of an agent's license once it is revoked?

A. Pending
B. Cancelled
C. Breached
D. Suspended

**35.** Which insurance policy provides extra liability coverage for the insured party?

A. Umbrella policy
B. Home insurance
C. Flood insurance
D. Hazard insurance

**36.** What is never included in the process of valuation?

A. Comparative Market Analysis
B. Appraisal
C. Location
D. Condition of the house

**37.** What type of contract allows the parties involved to disaffirm without liability?

A. Bilateral contract
B. Implied contract
C. Unilateral contract
D. Voidable Contract

**38.** What fiduciary duty does a broker neglect by failing to disclosing the buyer's inability to afford a down payment?

A. Obedience
B. Disclosure
C. Accountability
D. Confidentiality

**39.** James and Peter co-own a property where they both have equal undivided interests and right of survivorship. What co-ownership agreement do they have?

A. Tenancy in entirety
B. Joint tenancy
C. Tenancy in common
D. Tenancy at will

**40.** What is an exclusive term to describe the lease entered when an individual buys shares from a housing corporation?

A. Percentage lease
B. Gross lease
C. Net lease
D. Proprietary lease

**41.** What is the state of having no legal effect?

    A. Enforceable
    B. Cancelled
    C. Void
    D. Terminated

**42.** How many square feet constitute an acre?

    A. 25,235
    B. 43,560
    C. 50,525
    D. 70,000

**43.** What is the set minimum amp for a new construction?

    A. 100 amps
    B. 150 amps
    C. 200 amps
    D. 250 amps

**44.** What is the debt-to-equity ratio on a mortgage valued at $1,000,000 with a loan of $750,000?

    A. 25%
    B. 50%
    C. 65%
    D. 75%

**45.** Who controls flood insurance?

    A. FEMA
    B. EPA
    C. CERCLA
    D. FHA

**46.** What is a detailed building plan that is needed before starting construction?

    A. Building design
    B. Execution plan
    C. Blueprint
    D. Authorized plan

**47.** What type of house insulation was banned due to the release of formaldehyde fumes?

    A. Foam boards
    B. Loose fill
    C. Vapor barriers
    D. UFFI

**48.** What is the term used to describe a scenario where an agent represents both the buyer and the seller?

    A. Single agency
    B. Dual agency
    C. Multi agency
    D. Representing both agency

**49.** Which formal agreement gives an agent the sole right to sell a property?

- A. Purchase agreement
- B. Floating rate
- C. Exclusive Right-to-Sell Agreement
- D. Bridge loan

**50.** A tenant is legally allowed to remove equipment previously installed to facilitate business operations before the expiry of a lease. Why is this the case?

- A. The equipment is considered trade fixtures
- B. The equipment belongs to the lease holder
- C. The lessor does not want it
- D. It was part of the lease agreement

**51.** What type of easement attaches rights to an individual rather than the property?

- A. Easement appurtenant
- B. Easement in gross
- C. Prescriptive easement
- D. All of the above

**52.** What is the name given to the lowest section of the roof that extends into the sidewalls?

- A. Board
- B. Eaves
- C. Joists
- D. Beams

**53.** Which two parties are responsible for determining the commission earned by the broker?

- A. Seller and agent
- B. Seller and broker
- C. Buyer and agent
- D. Buyer and seller

**54.** Why must a lawsuit be filed within a specific time after an occurrence?

- A. To prevent the criminal from getting away
- B. Lis pendens
- C. Credibility
- D. Statute of limitations

**55.** Chris borrows money to purchase a new home and gives the mortgage to the lender as security. What term can be used to refer to Chris?

- A. Mortgagor
- B. Mortgagee
- C. Broker
- D. Buyer

**56.** What type of lease does a tenant have when he is paying a percentage of gross sales in addition to the base rent?

- A. Proprietary lease
- B. Net lease
- C. Percentage lease
- D. Gross lease

**57.** Why was the Civil Rights Act of 1866 significant in real estate?

- A. It protected against racial discrimination
- B. It protected interests of women
- C. It protected children's rights
- D. It protected against ageism

**58.** Why was the Privacy Act of 1974 significant?

- A. It required agencies to publicize records to the Federal Register
- B. It required privacy of records
- C. It required federal government to operate without transparency
- D. It required credit information to be kept private

**59.** Why was the Fair Housing Act of 1968 significant?

- A. It prohibited agents from asking prospective buyers about income
- B. It prohibited discrimination when selling, financing, or renting of a property
- C. It created affordable housing for low-income citizens
- D. None of the above

**60.** Jack is trying to convince Mary to sell her property in her neighborhood because it is changing due to the influx of people of other ethnic backgrounds. What is he doing?

- A. Steering
- B. Discriminating
- C. Blockbusting
- D. Convincing

**61.** What is the name of an agreement that allows for conditions on a property?

- A. Contract
- B. Deed
- C. Lease
- D. Qualified fee estate

**62.** What is **redlining**?

- A. Refusal by lending institutions to grant loans based on race
- B. Refusal by lending institutions to grant loans to people with poor credit scores
- C. Refusal of lending institutions to grant loans based on the agency being used for a purchase
- D. Refusal of a lending institution to make a loan because the area is integrated or populated by culturally diverse people

**63.** What is a form of co-ownership that involves a husband and wife having equal and undivided interest in the property?

- A. Joint tenancy
- B. Tenancy in common
- C. Tenancy by entirety
- D. Tenancy at will

**64.** What is the act of a property reverting to the state on death of the owner?

- A. Escheat
- B. Encumbrance
- C. Easement
- D. Suing

**65.** If you have a loan of $150,000 with an 8% interest, how much do you pay in interest every month?

    A. $1,000
    B. $1,200
    C. $5,000
    D. $12,000

**66.** Based on their contract, a lender declares the entire balance of the loan due immediately due to default by the borrower. How is this possible?

    A. Payday loans
    B. Alternative financing
    C. Acceleration clause
    D. Lines of credit

**67.** What type of payment plan allows a borrower to make smaller payments in the early years of a mortgage with payments increasing over time?

    A. Blanket mortgage
    B. Graduated mortgage
    C. Anomalous mortgage
    D. Balloon mortgage

**68.** What kind of mortgage should you apply for if you are buying more than an individual unit or plot?

    A. Graduated mortgage
    B. Blanket mortgage
    C. Balloon mortgage
    D. Adjustable rate mortgage

**69.** A salesperson is presented with two offers on a listed property. One is above the listing price and another below, which offer should he present to the seller?

    A. Both offers
    B. The one above the listing price
    C. The one below the listing price
    D. Neither

**70.** What is the name of a transaction where a seller finances the whole sale or part of the sale of a property for the buyer?

    A. Mortgage
    B. Refinancing
    C. Purchase money
    D. Buydown

**71.** What is an assessment of the value of a property as of a specific date based on objective data?

    A. CMA
    B. Listing price
    C. Tax value
    D. Appraisal

**72.** Which toxic metallic element is found in old paint and water pipes?

    A. Mercury
    B. Manganese
    C. Cadmium
    D. Lead

73. What is the amount of space used to calculate the lease payments which includes the shared property's common and service areas?

    A. Rentable square footage
    B. Usable square footage
    C. Common areas
    D. Service areas

74. Which chemical compounds commonly used in coolants and refrigeration contribute to the depletion of the ozone?

    A. CFCs
    B. Tetrafluoroethane
    C. Anhydrous ammonia
    D. Greenhouse gases

75. Which of the following does liability insurance protect you from?

    A. House fire
    B. Injury incurred on property
    C. Flood
    D. All of the above

76. What is a deed used for?

    A. To transfer title rights
    B. An official document proving a bank has loaned money
    C. A pro forma statement
    D. A lien

77. What is the measurement used to show the volatility of a market?

    A. Absorption rate
    B. Fluctuation rate
    C. Inflation
    D. Purchase deviation

78. What is the relationship between a broker and their client called?

    A. Fiduciary
    B. Trustee
    C. Seller disclosure
    D. Subagent

79. What is the law of agency?

    A. Commissions that are collected from both parties
    B. A set of laws that apply to a person who acts on behalf of another person
    C. The ability to accept an offer on behalf of the seller
    D. An authorized agency selling another's property

80. A severance is defined as _____.

    A. Real property that is converted into personal property
    B. Anything that is attached to the property naturally or by a person
    C. A person that is acting under a power of attorney
    D. An agreement between a lender and a borrower in which the borrower pledges collateral on a loan

**THIS IS THE END OF THE NATIONAL PORTION.**

## State Portion

1. The Michigan Marketable Title Act disregards title defects older than _____ .

   A. 35 years
   B. 40 years
   C. 45 years
   D. 50 years

2. This international organization is a group of real estate license law officials that regulates more than 2 million licensees.

   A. Association of Real Estate License Law Official (ARELLO)
   B. International Real Estate License Law
   C. Real Estate License Law Official
   D. There is no such organization

3. In Michigan, adverse possession can be obtained if the person has occupied the property for _____ .

   A. 22 years
   B. 20 years
   C. 15 years
   D. 10 years

4. Which of the following is required for a person to become a salesperson in Michigan?

   A. 40 hours of approved pre-licensing education
   B. College degree
   C. 300 hours of internship with a licensed salesperson
   D. All of the above

**5.** Which of the following states does Michigan have reciprocity with?

    A. Pennsylvania
    B. Idaho
    C. California
    D. None of the above

**6.** In Michigan a _____ is written governmental permission that allows use of property inconsistent with zoning but necessary for the common good.

    A. Special use permit
    B. Conditional-use permit
    C. Special zoning permission
    D. Conditional zoning permit

**7.** What is a contingency?

    A. A provision that requires a certain act to be done for a certain event to occur prior to a contract being binding
    B. A provision that requires an additional fee before a contract to be binding
    C. A provision that a licensee must comply with according to the board
    D. None of the above

**8.** In Michigan, a landlord is required to return a tenant's security deposit within _____ of termination of the lease.

    A. 1 year
    B. 6 months
    C. 30 days
    D. 90 days

9. What is the maximum property value that may be designated homestead?

   A. $10,000
   B. $3,500
   C. $5,000
   D. $7,500

10. Michigan law prohibits housing discrimination on the basis of _____.

   A. Height
   B. Weight
   C. National origin
   D. All of the above

11. A property owner builds a fence around their property. The neighbor of the property owner begins to use the fence as a method to restrain their dog. What must the neighbor do?

   A. The neighbor does not have to do anything
   B. The neighbor must compensate the property owner for their proportionate share of the fence
   C. The neighbor must gain permission from the fence's property owner
   D. The neighbor must build their own fence

12. Who is empowered to resolve disputes involving fences in Michigan?

   A. Attorneys
   B. Michigan Board of Real Estate and Salesperson
   C. Local government
   D. State government

**13.** A fence viewer is responsible for which of the following?

    A.   Determining responsibility for cost of construction
    B.   Assessing boundaries
    C.   Resolving disputes regarding damage to fences
    D.   All of the above

**14.** Which of the following statements is true about rental deposits in Michigan?

    A.   The deposit limit is 1 month's rent
    B.   Interest on the deposit is not required
    C.   The landlord must supply the tenant with a checklist of damages upon termination of the lease
    D.   All of the above

**15.** Which of the following is not required to become a real estate broker in Michigan?

    A.   5 years of full-time real estate salesperson experience
    B.   96 hours of broker licensing education
    C.   High school diploma
    D.   All of the above are requirements

**16.** The _____ was created to license and regulate the practice of real estate brokers and salespersons.

    A.   Michigan Board of Real Estate Brokers and Salespersons
    B.   Real Estate License and Regulation Board
    C.   Commission of Real Estate
    D.   Board of Real Estate Licensing and Regulation

**17.** According to Michigan homestead laws, what other types of property cannot be seized by creditors?

   A. Household goods
   B. Limited quantity of livestock, poultry, and grain
   C. Money or benefits from certain insurance or disability policies
   D. All of the above

**18.** Which of the following types of real estate licenses do not have to be renewed in Michigan?

   A. Real estate broker
   B. Real estate broker company
   C. Branch office
   D. All of the above must be renewed

**19.** What is the right of redemption period in Michigan?

   A. 1 year
   B. 6 months
   C. 3 months
   D. 2 years

**20.** Who appoints the members of the Board of Real Estate Brokers and Salespersons?

   A. A public vote
   B. The other board members
   C. The governor
   D. State senate

21. Applicants for the broker license must compete _____ hours of education in the state of Michigan.

    A.  90
    B.  100
    C.  200
    D.  60

22. A _____ is a broker license that is issued to a legal entity that is able to do business in the state of Michigan.

    A.  Business broker license
    B.  Broker as non-living entities
    C.  Entity broker
    D.  Corporation entity

23. An applicant is denied a salesperson license. What can the applicant do?

    A.  Reapply for the licensure
    B.  Petition the department and board
    C.  Send letters of reference to the board
    D.  The applicant must wait 2 years to reapply

24. In Michigan, a licensed broker and salesperson must carry _____ when working in real estate.

    A.  A pocket card
    B.  Licenses
    C.  Brokerage information
    D.  A&B only

**25.** Tenant does not pay rent for property he is renting. What is the statute of limitations for collection of rent in Michigan?

A. 2 years
B. 10 years
C. 6 years
D. 1 year

**26.** Michigan requires how many hours of continuing education?

A. 6 hours a year
B. 18 hours a year
C. 30 hours a year
D. 5 hours a year

**27.** Which of the following is a responsibility of the Department of Licensing and Regulatory Affairs (LARA)?

A. Issue licenses to qualifying applicants
B. Review complaints against licensees
C. Revoke or suspend licenses of builders, brokers or salespersons who have violated the civil rights act
D. A&C only

**28.** Brokers as entity must have _____.

A. 2 licensed brokers
B. A licensed attorney
C. 1 living licensed principal associate broker
D. None of the above

29. An owner or an officer of an entity that is legally able to do business in the state is called a _____.

   A. Principal associate broker
   B. Senior broker
   C. Managing broker
   D. Licensed broker

30. Applicants for a broker or salesperson license must do which of the following?

   A. Intern with a licensed broker
   B. Submit to a criminal record or submit other requested information
   C. Be 25 years of age
   D. All of the above

31. In Michigan, what is the maximum acreage that can be designated as homestead in a rural setting?

   A. 40 acres
   B. 1 lot
   C. 2 lots
   D. 75 acres

32. The Michigan Board of Real Estate Brokers and Salespersons has the power to do which of the following?

   A. Hold formal and informal hearing to address accusations of misconduct and grievances.
   B. Hold conference for licensed brokers and salespersons
   C. Conduct an investigation to respond to a complaint or problem
   D. All of the above

**33.** What is a branch office license?

    A. A license required to open offices in different states

    B. A license required for a principal brokerage location

    C. A license required for any brokerage location

    D. None of the above

**34.** How many members are on the Michigan Board of Real Estate Brokers and Salespersons?

    A. 9 members

    B. 10 members

    C. 6 members

    D. 11 members

**35.** Which statement is true about adverse possession in the state of Michigan?

    A. Adverse possession is controlled by state law

    B. A person can obtain adverse possession even if they are a trespasser

    C. The occupant does not have to hold the title to the property

    D. All of the above

**THIS IS THE END OF THE STATE PORTION.**

# Answer Key – National Portion

| | | | | | | | |
|---|---|---|---|---|---|---|---|
| 1. | A | 21. | A | 41. | C | 61. | D |
| 2. | B | 22. | A | 42. | B | 62. | D |
| 3. | B | 23. | B | 43. | A | 63. | C |
| 4. | A | 24. | D | 44. | D | 64. | A |
| 5. | D | 25. | C | 45. | A | 65. | A |
| 6. | B | 26. | C | 46. | C | 66. | C |
| 7. | C | 27. | C | 47. | D | 67. | B |
| 8. | D | 28. | A | 48. | B | 68. | B |
| 9. | A | 29. | D | 49. | C | 69. | A |
| 10. | B | 30. | B | 50. | A | 70. | C |
| 11. | B | 31. | D | 51. | B | 71. | D |
| 12. | A | 32. | A | 52. | B | 72. | D |
| 13. | A | 33. | A | 53. | B | 73. | A |
| 14. | C | 34. | D | 54. | D | 74. | A |
| 15. | D | 35. | A | 55. | A | 75. | D |
| 16. | A | 36. | A | 56. | C | 76. | A |
| 17. | B | 37. | D | 57. | A | 77. | A |
| 18. | C | 38. | B | 58. | A | 78. | A |
| 19. | C | 39. | B | 59. | B | 79. | B |
| 20. | D | 40. | D | 60. | C | 80. | A |

1. **A) A loan that has a predetermined repayment interest rate**

Commonly compared to floating rate, which is a loan that uses external factors as a benchmark for interest rates and is usually fluctuating based on the external market.

2. **B) Civil Rights Act of 1866**

This act declares all citizens equal and under the protection of the law. The law emphasized protecting all citizens of African descent during the Civil War.

3. **B) Promissory note**

This is a financial document by the issuer to the payee that contains a promise to make payment for a definite sum of money. It is usually valid for payment either on demand or on a specified date. It usually contains information regarding the principal amount, interest rate, date and place of issuance, maturity date and signature of the parties involved.

4.    **A) Refinancing**

This is the process of replacing an existing mortgage with another that offers more favorable terms to the borrower. Refinancing enables a borrower to negotiate for lower monthly payments, lower interest rates and renegotiate the loan payment term.

5.    **D) All of the above**

An appurtenance is real property fixed to the land that is passed along with the sale of a property.

6.    **B) Certificate of deposit**

This is a product offered by banks and credit facilities to customers enabling them to deposit a lump sum amount for a predetermined period with an agreed upon interest rate premium. Doing some research on the certificate of deposit terms offered by the different available facilities is important to yield better returns.

7.    **C) $250,000**

$225,000 / (1 - 0.1) = $250,000

8.    **D) Annual percentage rate**

This is the annual rate charged on a loan or investment. It is usually used to express the actual annual cost of funds over the lifespan of a loan or cash investment. As loan arrangements vary among institutions and the situation surrounding the loan, a standardized APR is set to protect borrowers from unreasonably high interest rates.

9.    **A) Public auctions**

Homes are usually put on auction due to default on a mortgage or property taxes. Buying a house at an auction is risky as it often does not give the buyer a chance to view the interior of the house. When buying a property at an auction, it is necessary to run background research on the property.

10.    **B) Pre-qualification**

These is the process of reviewing clients' creditworthiness and is usually used as a marketing strategy to obtain new clients. Creditors usually mail a potential borrower outlining maximum limit for loan.

11.    **B) Power of attorney**

This is a legal document that transfers rights to act in place of a principal in the event that they are unable to act for themselves. The terms of the contract usually include what can be managed and where the power of the agent ends.

12.    **A) Exclusive listing**

An exclusive listing is an agreement between a seller and an agent stating that commission on a sale can only be earned when a sale is made within a specified period of time. The timeframe for the sale is usually agreed on by both parties while entering the agreement.

13.    **A) Single agency**

This is brokerage agreement where a buying agent is assigned the role to represent a buyer and works in single agency capacity as the buyer's agent. This agent is bound by fiduciary duties to the buyer and cannot disclose any confidential information to the other party.

14.    **C) Arms-length transaction**

This is a transaction where both the buyer and the seller are acting in self-interest with an aim of getting the better deal. The discrepancy is usually solved when both parties agree on a middle ground that fulfills the interests of both the buyer and the seller.

15.    **D) Adjustment date**

This is the changing of a date where calculations on items such as property taxes, rent and damage deposits are done.

16.    **A) Assumable mortgage**

This is a mortgage arrangement that allows the seller to transfer the terms and conditions of a mortgage to a buyer. In this case, a buyer absorbs the seller's remaining debt instead of taking out a new mortgage.

17.    **B) Call option**

This is a contract signed by both the buyer and the seller giving one party the right to sell and the other the right to buy a property on a future date. The price of the property is usually included in the contract and remains the same regardless of inflation or market shifts.

18.    **C) A specified expiration date**

An exclusive listing contract is an agreement where a real estate agent receives commission within a specified amount of time. The agent receives commission no matter how the buyer is found.

19. **C) Reciprocity**

Real estate license reciprocity allows agents to obtain a real estate license in another state by taking the reciprocal state's exam.

20. **D) Privacy**

The 6 fiduciary duties of a real estate agent are: **O**bedience, **L**oyalty, **D**isclosure, **C**onfidentiality, **A**ccountability, and **R**easonable care / diligence (OLDCAR)

21. **A) Conditions that must be met by both the buyer and the seller before closing**

They are set in place to protect the parties involved in the contract. A breach in the contingencies results in the immediate termination of the contract.

22. **A) Any individual whose name appears on the loan document**

This is often someone whose credit score was taken into consideration when determining whether or not a loan can be extended. A co-borrower can be beneficial for a borrower that is unable to get favorable interest rates.

23. **B) Construction loan**

This is a short-term loan that is usually taken to finance the construction of a home or real estate property. It is usually taken to provide cash flow before larger funding is approved.

24. **D) Final walkthrough**

This is a visit done to the property by the buyer after all financing has been secured. A buyer is required to visit the premise and establish whether all the things that were discussed in the contract have been met prior to closing the deal.

25. **C) Fixed mortgage rate**

This is a mortgage loan whose interest rate remains the same throughout the longevity of the loan.

26. **C) Loan to value ratio**

This is defined as the percentage of the home's value owned by the borrower after making a down payment. It is calculated by taking the mortgage loan amount and dividing it by the appraisal value of the property being bought. The higher the loan to value ratio, the less likely lenders are to agree to loans.

27. **C) 20%**

($1,000 * 12) / $60,000 = 0.2

28. **A) Vicarious liability**

This is a secondary form of liability where a superior is held accountable for the actions of his subordinates. In the real estate sector, vicarious liability arises when an agent hired by either the buyer or seller acts inappropriately. In this case, the client is held accountable for the misconduct of his agent.

29. **D) Agency disclosure statement**

This is a statement signed by both the seller and buyer prior to the real estate transaction. Its role is to disclose the role of the agent in the transaction. An agent can either be a broker for either the buyer or the seller, a dual agent or a sub agent. In order to enforce disclosure laws, some states have a disclosure form written into law.

30. **B) Price fixing**

This is a situation that arises where a number of real estate agencies that dominate the market agree on a set commission. Brokers are required by law to set their individual commissions where consideration to the market going rate is allowed. Choosing to agree on a set standard commission could result in the suspension of a broker's license. These laws were set in place to protect the buyers and sellers in the market.

31. **D) IRS**

The IRS uses the general rule that an individual can be classified as an independent contractor if the payer has the right to control the result of work and not how it will be done.

32. **A) Freehold**

Freehold title is a title given to a freehold property where the owner owns the unit and the land on which the establishment has been developed and anything that is erected on the land.

33. **A) $0**

According to the Taxpayer Relief Act of 1997, a married couple is eligible for exemption from capital gain tax on profits of up to $500,000. This can only be claimed provided the property is the primary home of the selling couple meaning they have been living there for at least 2 years. Therefore, Mr. and Mrs. Smith do not owe anything in capital gain tax.

34. **D) Suspended**

He can choose to wait for the suspension to be lifted or look for another broker. A license can be suspended due to violation of insurance laws, providing materially misleading information and fraudulent practices. A revoked can only be reinstated after one year with undeniable evidence of trustworthiness and ability to uphold the law.

35.    **A) Umbrella policy**

An umbrella insurance policy is an excess liability policy that is often used as a fail-safe for assets and savings. It is mostly used by people that are at risk of being sued. Contrary to popular belief, an umbrella policy does not cover additional risk area but acts as an addition to an already existing insurance.

36.    **A) Comparative Market Analysis**

Comparative Market Analysis is never used in valuation as it is based on the market value of similar properties whereas no two real properties are alike.

37.    **D) Voidable Contract**

A voidable contract is a formal agreement between parties that can be rendered obsolete due to legal factors. Some of the factors that can result in a voidable contract being rejected are fraud, undisclosed facts and a breach of the contract. A voidable contract is always considered legal unless rendered unenforceable.

38.    **B) Disclosure**

Fiduciary duties arise when an agency operates on behalf of a client. In this case the agent is legally mandated to act in the best interest of the client. When an agent fails to disclose facts that may influence the final decision of the client, he is in violation of the disclosure clause.

39.    **B) Joint tenancy**

A joint tenancy is an arrangement where two or more parties agree to co-own a property with equal rights and obligations. Upon death of a partner, the property remains solely in the ownership of the surviving partner. A joint tenancy has to be entered at the same time through a deed. Joint tenancy has the advantage of avoiding legal battles after the demise of a partner but can be hard to settle in the event of a divorced couple.

40.    **D) Proprietary lease**

A proprietary lease is a is an agreement that allows a shareholder in a housing corporation to live in a unit equaling their stakes in the corporation. A shareholder does not buy the property but shares in the corporation. In this case, the shares act as collateral on the lease.

41.    **C) Void**

This means to be obsolete and have no enforceable terms. Parties to a void contract are not bound by its terms making the contract unenforceable.

34

42. **B) 43,560**

An acre is a standard unit for measuring land. An acre does not have to be square shaped but contains an equivalent of 43560 square feet.

43. **A) 100 amps**

The minimum is 100 amps as anything below that may not be able to sustain the electric needs of a home. Larger homes can have between 150 and 200 amps based on the type of electronic systems installed. Having a proper electrical distribution in the home will also avoid trips.

44. **D) 75%**

750,000 / 1,000,000 = 0.75

The debt-to-equity ratio is used to determine whether a buyer can afford a house or to refinance an already owned property.

45. **A) FEMA**

The Federal Emergency Management Agency focuses on promoting the need to work together to support citizens and fast respondents. Its goal is to ensure citizens build and sustain to prepare for and recover from calamities.

46. **C) Blueprint**

A blueprint is a reproduction of a technical drawing on a light sensitive sheet that is done using a contact printer. A blueprint is usually required to predetermine the design and pattern that is going to be followed in a construction.

47. **D) UFFI**

Urea Formaldehyde Foam Insulation was used for house insulation in the 70s due to its high thermal resistance. Testing in the lab showed that the insulation produced fumes that were toxic for humans and the environment leading to its ban in 1982.

48. **B) Dual agency**

Dual agency is legal in Pennsylvania provided both the buyer and the seller agree to the arrangement after pros and cons of the relationship are laid on the table. Opting to have a dual agent means that the client cannot expect the agent to act in their best interest as he is representing two conflicting interests.

49.  **C) Exclusive Right-to-Sell Agreement**

This is an agreement between a seller and agent granting the agent or firm the exclusive right to market and sell a property.

50.  **A) The equipment is considered trade fixtures**

Trade fixtures are removable personal property that are installed in a leased space to facilitate business running. For one to be allowed to remove a fixture, it must be essential for the running of the business to not cause damage to the property and be removed before the expiry of the lease.

51.  **B) Easement in gross**

The rights associated by the easement are irrevocable for the person granted. A transfer of the property to another individual through sale or inheritance does not warrant an automatic transfer of the rights to the new owner. This renders the easement of gross void.

52.  **B) Eaves**

An eave is the lower edge of a roof that protrude or hangs over the building's side.

53.  **B) Seller and broker**

The seller and broker are usually responsible for agreeing in the amount of commission that should be paid to the broker

54.  **D) Statute of limitations**

The statute of limitations is a law that sets the maximum period of time parties involved in a rift have to initiate legal proceedings from the day of the occurrence of the event. The time allocated to offences differs according to the nature of the offence.

55.  **A) Mortgagor**

A mortgagor is an individual that borrows money from a lender in order to purchase a property. The lending is based on the individual's credit score and collateral. A title must be handed to the lender as collateral for the loan.

56.  **C) Percentage lease**

A percentage lease is a type of lease where the tenant pays rent plus a percentage of any revenue earned while doing business on the property. This agreement significantly reduces the rent paid. The parties involved agree on a base point where percentage lease kicks in.

**57.** **A) It protected against racial discrimination**

The Civil Rights act of 1866 banned racial discrimination in real estate and housing transactions. People of any race had equal rights as whites to buy, sell, or lease property.

**58.** **A) It required agencies to publicize records to the Federal Register**

The Privacy Act of 1974 is an act that established code of fair information maintenance governing the collection, use and maintenance of individuals that is maintained by federal agencies. The act required the agencies to publicize the records in the Federal Register.

**59.** **B) It prohibited discrimination when selling, financing, or renting of a property**

The 1968 Act prohibited discrimination based on race, religion, national origin, sex, handicap and family status of the sale, financing, and rental of housing.

**60.** **C) Blockbusting**

This is the act of trying to manipulate tenants to sell or rent their properties at lower rates due to an influx of minority groups in a once segregated neighborhood.

**61.** **D) Qualified fee estate**

This is an estate agreement that facilitates the grantor to propose a set of conditions. A breach in the condition limitation may result in termination of the agreement. A quality fee estate can also be based on the occurrence of a predetermined event.

**62.** **D) Refusal of a lending institution to make a loan because the area is integrated or populated by culturally diverse people**

This usually occurs when a lending institution has a map of areas they would not like to initiate credit in. Potential property owners are denied mortgages despite great credit scores due to the location of the property they intend to purchase.

**63.** **C) Tenancy by entirety**

Only married couples can enter this type of co-ownership where the property is jointly owned as a single entity. It facilitates right of survivorship and can be terminated upon death of spouse or divorce.

**64.** **A) Escheat**

A property can be reverted to the state if no claimants have come forth to claim the property or the available heir has been deemed legally unfit to be granted ownership. It is revocable once a legal heir claims the property.

65. **A) $1,000**

($150,000 * 0.08) / 12 = $1,000

66. **C) Acceleration clause**

This is a contract that allows a lender to require full settlement of an outstanding loan due to a breach of predetermined conditions.

67. **B) Graduated mortgage**

This is a fixed price loan that allows the borrower to make smaller payments on the loan in the earlier payment years and continues to increase gradually until the mortgage is paid off. It considers individuals who were otherwise not qualified for the higher rate to qualify.

68. **B) Blanket mortgage**

A blanket mortgage is a mortgage that covers two or more pieces of real estate. The real estate property is held as collateral. Individual properties can be sold without having to retire the mortgage. This insurance is usually taken when purchasing and developing land.

69. **A) Both offers**

The agent is required by fiduciary duties to present both the offers to the client. Choosing to present the higher offer to the client in order to reap higher commission from the sale is a breach of fiduciary duties.

70. **C) Purchase money**

This is a mortgage issued by the seller as part of a real estate transaction. This arrangement is usually reached when the buyer is not eligible for the traditional mortgage. A down payment is usually placed on the property as an order of the financial transaction.

71. **D) Appraisal**

An appraisal is an opinion usually given by a professional on the market value of a property. Properties usually require an appraisal is unique and market value of similar properties may not offer an accurate value of the property.

72. **D) Lead**

Lead is a periodic metal that was used in paint in the 1970s as it accelerated drying, maintained a fresh appearance and resisted moisture. Older plumbing systems used lead lines and water often corroded the material as it was transported to the consumer's taps. Use of lead in paint was discontinued as it was found to cause nervous system damage and stunted growth in children.

73. **A) Rentable square footage**

Rentable square footage is inclusive of the usable square footage and common areas. The price per rentable square foot is usually calculated using a pro-rata calculation based on the size of the space being leased.

74. **A) CFCs**

CFCs are nonflammable chemicals that are commonly used in aerosol sprays and industrial cleaning products. Once these chemicals are released into the atmosphere they rise into the stratosphere where ultraviolet rays from the sun break them down. This breakdown releases chlorine atoms that destroy ozone molecules therefore forming ozone holes.

75. **D) All of the above**

Liability insurance covers everything from house fires, injuries incurred on the property, floods, injured domestic workers, falling trees, and more.

76. **A) To transfer title rights**

The buyer and seller must both sign a deed to transfer the property's ownership.

77. **A) Absorption rate**

This is a ration of the number of properties that have been sold against the number of properties that are available for sale within a specified area.

78. **A) Fiduciary**

Fiduciary is the relationship between client and broker. An agent is the fiduciary of the client.

79. **B) A set of laws that apply to a person who acts on behalf of another person**

The law of agency is a set of duties that real estate professionals owe to their clients, including disclosures that must be made to the client. These duties are set by each state.

80. **A) Real property that is converted into personal property**

There are two types of severance, actual severance and constructive severance. An actual severance is when an item is removed from the land and a constructive severance is when an item is detached by intent.

## Answer Key – State Portion

| | | | |
|---|---|---|---|
| 1. | B | 21. | A |
| 2. | A | 22. | B |
| 3. | C | 23. | B |
| 4. | A | 24. | D |
| 5. | D | 25. | C |
| 6. | B | 26. | A |
| 7. | A | 27. | D |
| 8. | C | 28. | C |
| 9. | B | 29. | A |
| 10. | D | 30. | B |
| 11. | B | 31. | A |
| 12. | C | 32. | D |
| 13. | D | 33. | C |
| 14. | D | 34. | A |
| 15. | A | 35. | D |
| 16. | A | | |
| 17. | D | | |
| 18. | D | | |
| 19. | B | | |
| 20. | C | | |

1.  **B) 40 years**

    This law disregards title defects that are older that 40 years. It acts as a statute of limitations.

2.  **A) Association of Real Estate License Law Official (ARELLO)**

    This is an international organization that facilitate the exchange of ideas and cooperation among real estate.

3.  **C) 15 years**

    In Michigan, a person can obtain adverse obsession after 15 years of occupancy. This allows the occupant to become the legal owner of the property.

4.  **A) 40 hours of approved pre-licensing education**

    The education must be successfully completed. They must also pass the final course exam and select a sponsoring broker.

5.  **D) None of the above**

    Michigan has no reciprocity with any state but a licensee in another state may qualify for licensure in Michigan if they have experience and training equal to that required in Michigan.

6.  **B) Conditional-use permit**

    This gives permission to use land that is inconsistent with zoning laws but is necessary for the common good. Examples of this is an emergency medical facility in a predominantly residential area.

7.  **A) A provision that requires a certain act to be done for a certain event to occur prior to a contract being binding**

    A contingency is in a contract that requires an act to be done for another event to happen and before a contract can become binding.

8.  **C) 30 days**

    Within 30 days of the termination of the lease, a landlord is required to return the security deposit to the tenant.

9.  **B) $3,500**

    A maximum property value for the Homestead act, in Michigan, is 3,500 dollars. The value cannot exceed that amount.

10. **D) All of the above**

    Michigan housing laws prohibits housing discrimination based on all of the above as well as race, sex, color, sex, and marital status. The exemption to this law is housing programs for elderly that restrict children to certain areas of the complex.

11. **B) The neighbor must compensate the property owner for their proportionate share of the fence**

    In the case of a neighbor using another neighbor's property fence to restrain an animal or animals, the neighbor must compensate the property owner for a proportionate share of the fence.

12. **C) Local government**

    Michigan law has provided local governments with the power to resolve disputes involving fences efficiently.

13. **D) All of the above**

The fence viewer is appointed by the township and is responsible for all of the above.

14. **D) All of the above**

All of the above are true regarding rental deposits in the state of Michigan.

15. **A) 5 years of full-time real estate salesperson experience**

5 years of salesperson experience is not required. Michigan only requires 3 years of salesperson experience.

16. **A) Michigan Board of Real Estate Brokers and Salespersons**

This organization was created in 1980 and defines a real estate broker as an individual or an entity that provides real estate services.

17. **D) All of the above**

All of the above are items that cannot be seized by creditors but there are some exceptions to this rule in cases of divorce or child and spousal support.

18. **D) All of the above must be renewed**

All of the above licenses must be renewed. A real estate salesperson license must be renewed as well.

19. **B) 6 months**

The redemption period starts the day of the sheriff's sale and is 6 months long for most types of mortgage.

20. **C) The governor**

The board members are appointed by the governor and consists of 9 people 3 of whom represent the public.

21. **A) 90**

To become a broker, the applicant must complete 90 hours of approved schooling, with 9 of them on civil rights. The education must also be completed within 36 months of the application unless the applicant held an active license in the interim.

22.  **B) Broker as non-living entities**

This is when a broker license is issued to an individual or a corporation, partnership, limited liability company or another type of legal entity able to do business in Michigan. A salesperson license and an associate broker's license may not be issued to them.

23.  **B) Petition the department and board**

The petition must be in writing and the department and board with review the decision.

24.  **D) A&B only**

Michigan requires licensees to carry their license and pocket card with them when working in real estate.

25.  **C) 6 years**

The statute of limitations for a landlord to collect rent from a tenant is 6 years. It is 2 years for personal injuries and 10 years for judgments.

26.  **A) 6 hours a year**

Licensees must complete 6 hours of continuing education a year, 2 of those hours being core classes.

27.  **D) A&C only**

The Department of Licensing and Regulatory Affairs, or LARA, is responsible for issuing licenses and for revoking or suspending licenses of builders, salespersons and brokers who have violated the civil rights act.

28.  **C) 1 living licensed principal associate broker**

This type of brokerage must have a living licensed principal associate broker.

29.  **A) Principal associate broker**

This type of broker is a member or manager, owner or officer of a legal entity that is able to do business in the state of Michigan.

30.  **B) Submit to a criminal record or submit other requested information**

The applicant must submit to a criminal record or submit other requested information. The applicant must also be 18 years of age, not misrepresent a material fact on the application and pass a state approved examination.

31.     **A) 40 acres**

In a rural area the maximum acreage is 40 acres while in an urban area the maximum is one lot and the house on the lot in the plat.

32.     **D) All of the above**

The board has the power to revoke a license, conduct investigations, hold conference, and have formal and informal hearings.

33.     **C) A license required for any brokerage location**

This license is required for any branch location of a brokerage, this includes a principal location. A license is required to do business.

34.     **A) 9 members**

There are 9 members of the Michigan Board of Real Estate Brokers and Salespersons. 6 of those members are professional and 3 are public.

35.     **D) All of the above**

In Michigan, the occupant can be a trespasser and does not need to hold the title property. The doctrine of adverse possession is controlled by state law.

# Practice Test 2

Directions:

1.      You have a 3-hour time limit to complete the whole exam.

2.      To pass, you must answer at least 70% of all questions correctly.

3.      Some questions will require mathematics. You may use a calculator.

4.      **Phones and pagers are not allowed. Having either will result in automatic dismissal from the exam and nullification of exam scores.**

Tips:

- Answer all questions even if you are unsure.
- Mark any questions you are stuck on and revisit them after you are done. The exam is timed so make sure you finish as many questions as you can.
- After reading the question, try answering it in your head first to avoid getting confused by the choices.
- Read the entire question before looking at the answers.
- Use the process of elimination to filter out choices that don't seem correct to increase your chances of selecting the correct answer.
- Be aware of important keywords like **not, sometimes, always,** and **never**. These words completely alter the ask of the question so it's important to keep track of them.

**PLEASE READ THESE INSTRUCTIONS CAREFULLY.**

Name: _____          Date: _____

## NATIONAL PORTION

| | | | | |
|---|---|---|---|---|
| 1. | Ⓐ Ⓑ Ⓒ Ⓓ | 31. | Ⓐ Ⓑ Ⓒ Ⓓ | 61. Ⓐ Ⓑ Ⓒ Ⓓ |
| 2. | Ⓐ Ⓑ Ⓒ Ⓓ | 32. | Ⓐ Ⓑ Ⓒ Ⓓ | 62. Ⓐ Ⓑ Ⓒ Ⓓ |
| 3. | Ⓐ Ⓑ Ⓒ Ⓓ | 33. | Ⓐ Ⓑ Ⓒ Ⓓ | 63. Ⓐ Ⓑ Ⓒ Ⓓ |
| 4. | Ⓐ Ⓑ Ⓒ Ⓓ | 34. | Ⓐ Ⓑ Ⓒ Ⓓ | 64. Ⓐ Ⓑ Ⓒ Ⓓ |
| 5. | Ⓐ Ⓑ Ⓒ Ⓓ | 35. | Ⓐ Ⓑ Ⓒ Ⓓ | 65. Ⓐ Ⓑ Ⓒ Ⓓ |
| 6. | Ⓐ Ⓑ Ⓒ Ⓓ | 36. | Ⓐ Ⓑ Ⓒ Ⓓ | 66. Ⓐ Ⓑ Ⓒ Ⓓ |
| 7. | Ⓐ Ⓑ Ⓒ Ⓓ | 37. | Ⓐ Ⓑ Ⓒ Ⓓ | 67. Ⓐ Ⓑ Ⓒ Ⓓ |
| 8. | Ⓐ Ⓑ Ⓒ Ⓓ | 38. | Ⓐ Ⓑ Ⓒ Ⓓ | 68. Ⓐ Ⓑ Ⓒ Ⓓ |
| 9. | Ⓐ Ⓑ Ⓒ Ⓓ | 39. | Ⓐ Ⓑ Ⓒ Ⓓ | 69. Ⓐ Ⓑ Ⓒ Ⓓ |
| 10. | Ⓐ Ⓑ Ⓒ Ⓓ | 40. | Ⓐ Ⓑ Ⓒ Ⓓ | 70. Ⓐ Ⓑ Ⓒ Ⓓ |
| 11. | Ⓐ Ⓑ Ⓒ Ⓓ | 41. | Ⓐ Ⓑ Ⓒ Ⓓ | 71. Ⓐ Ⓑ Ⓒ Ⓓ |
| 12. | Ⓐ Ⓑ Ⓒ Ⓓ | 42. | Ⓐ Ⓑ Ⓒ Ⓓ | 72. Ⓐ Ⓑ Ⓒ Ⓓ |
| 13. | Ⓐ Ⓑ Ⓒ Ⓓ | 43. | Ⓐ Ⓑ Ⓒ Ⓓ | 73. Ⓐ Ⓑ Ⓒ Ⓓ |
| 14. | Ⓐ Ⓑ Ⓒ Ⓓ | 44. | Ⓐ Ⓑ Ⓒ Ⓓ | 74. Ⓐ Ⓑ Ⓒ Ⓓ |
| 15. | Ⓐ Ⓑ Ⓒ Ⓓ | 45. | Ⓐ Ⓑ Ⓒ Ⓓ | 75. Ⓐ Ⓑ Ⓒ Ⓓ |
| 16. | Ⓐ Ⓑ Ⓒ Ⓓ | 46. | Ⓐ Ⓑ Ⓒ Ⓓ | 76. Ⓐ Ⓑ Ⓒ Ⓓ |
| 17 | Ⓐ Ⓑ Ⓒ Ⓓ | 47. | Ⓐ Ⓑ Ⓒ Ⓓ | 77. Ⓐ Ⓑ Ⓒ Ⓓ |
| 18. | Ⓐ Ⓑ Ⓒ Ⓓ | 48. | Ⓐ Ⓑ Ⓒ Ⓓ | 78. Ⓐ Ⓑ Ⓒ Ⓓ |
| 19. | Ⓐ Ⓑ Ⓒ Ⓓ | 49. | Ⓐ Ⓑ Ⓒ Ⓓ | 79. Ⓐ Ⓑ Ⓒ Ⓓ |
| 20. | Ⓐ Ⓑ Ⓒ Ⓓ | 50. | Ⓐ Ⓑ Ⓒ Ⓓ | 80. Ⓐ Ⓑ Ⓒ Ⓓ |
| 21. | Ⓐ Ⓑ Ⓒ Ⓓ | 51. | Ⓐ Ⓑ Ⓒ Ⓓ | |
| 22. | Ⓐ Ⓑ Ⓒ Ⓓ | 52. | Ⓐ Ⓑ Ⓒ Ⓓ | |
| 23. | Ⓐ Ⓑ Ⓒ Ⓓ | 53. | Ⓐ Ⓑ Ⓒ Ⓓ | |
| 24. | Ⓐ Ⓑ Ⓒ Ⓓ | 54. | Ⓐ Ⓑ Ⓒ Ⓓ | |
| 25. | Ⓐ Ⓑ Ⓒ Ⓓ | 55. | Ⓐ Ⓑ Ⓒ Ⓓ | |
| 26. | Ⓐ Ⓑ Ⓒ Ⓓ | 56. | Ⓐ Ⓑ Ⓒ Ⓓ | |
| 27. | Ⓐ Ⓑ Ⓒ Ⓓ | 57. | Ⓐ Ⓑ Ⓒ Ⓓ | |
| 28. | Ⓐ Ⓑ Ⓒ Ⓓ | 58. | Ⓐ Ⓑ Ⓒ Ⓓ | |
| 29. | Ⓐ Ⓑ Ⓒ Ⓓ | 59. | Ⓐ Ⓑ Ⓒ Ⓓ | |
| 30. | Ⓐ Ⓑ Ⓒ Ⓓ | 60. | Ⓐ Ⓑ Ⓒ Ⓓ | |

# Practice Test 2

Name: _____                     Date: _____

## STATE PORTION

| | |
|---|---|
| 1. Ⓐ Ⓑ Ⓒ Ⓓ | 31. Ⓐ Ⓑ Ⓒ Ⓓ |
| 2. Ⓐ Ⓑ Ⓒ Ⓓ | 32. Ⓐ Ⓑ Ⓒ Ⓓ |
| 3. Ⓐ Ⓑ Ⓒ Ⓓ | 33. Ⓐ Ⓑ Ⓒ Ⓓ |
| 4. Ⓐ Ⓑ Ⓒ Ⓓ | 34. Ⓐ Ⓑ Ⓒ Ⓓ |
| 5. Ⓐ Ⓑ Ⓒ Ⓓ | 35. Ⓐ Ⓑ Ⓒ Ⓓ |
| 6. Ⓐ Ⓑ Ⓒ Ⓓ | |
| 7. Ⓐ Ⓑ Ⓒ Ⓓ | |
| 8. Ⓐ Ⓑ Ⓒ Ⓓ | |
| 9. Ⓐ Ⓑ Ⓒ Ⓓ | |
| 10. Ⓐ Ⓑ Ⓒ Ⓓ | |
| 11. Ⓐ Ⓑ Ⓒ Ⓓ | |
| 12. Ⓐ Ⓑ Ⓒ Ⓓ | |
| 13. Ⓐ Ⓑ Ⓒ Ⓓ | |
| 14. Ⓐ Ⓑ Ⓒ Ⓓ | |
| 15. Ⓐ Ⓑ Ⓒ Ⓓ | |
| 16. Ⓐ Ⓑ Ⓒ Ⓓ | |
| 17. Ⓐ Ⓑ Ⓒ Ⓓ | |
| 18. Ⓐ Ⓑ Ⓒ Ⓓ | |
| 19. Ⓐ Ⓑ Ⓒ Ⓓ | |
| 20. Ⓐ Ⓑ Ⓒ Ⓓ | |
| 21. Ⓐ Ⓑ Ⓒ Ⓓ | |
| 22. Ⓐ Ⓑ Ⓒ Ⓓ | |
| 23. Ⓐ Ⓑ Ⓒ Ⓓ | |
| 24. Ⓐ Ⓑ Ⓒ Ⓓ | |
| 25. Ⓐ Ⓑ Ⓒ Ⓓ | |
| 26. Ⓐ Ⓑ Ⓒ Ⓓ | |
| 27. Ⓐ Ⓑ Ⓒ Ⓓ | |
| 28. Ⓐ Ⓑ Ⓒ Ⓓ | |
| 29. Ⓐ Ⓑ Ⓒ Ⓓ | |
| 30. Ⓐ Ⓑ Ⓒ Ⓓ | |

# National Portion

1. What is the process of attempting to recover a loan from a borrower that has stopped making payments?

   A. Concession
   B. Final walk through
   C. Foreclosure
   D. Private mortgage insurance

2. What fibrous material causes cancer when released into the air?

   A. Asbestos
   B. Cotton
   C. Textiles
   D. Trunks

3. What are the vertical beams that frame the house?

   A. Frames
   B. Joists
   C. Shingles
   D. Studs

4. What is a reason a broker may be suspended or have their license revoked?

   A. Misrepresentation
   B. Failure to retain clients
   C. Failure to sell property within specified timeframe
   D. None of the above

5. A property manager makes routine rounds to repair air conditioning vents. What is the term used to refer to this?

   A. Aesthetic maintenance
   B. Avoiding depreciation
   C. Preventive maintenance
   D. Proration

6. What is another term that can be used to refer to the lender?

   A. Seller
   B. Mortgagee
   C. Mortgagor
   D. Loanee

7. If a seller nets $150,000 from the sale of her home, and the commission is 4%, how much did the home sell for?

   A. $144,000
   B. $148,500
   C. $156,000
   D. $156,250

8. What is the name given to the restriction of land usage by the local authorities?

   A. Building codes
   B. Denial
   C. Land zoning
   D. Property tax

9. What is the lender required to do once it is a borrower is unable to clear a mortgage?

    A. Threaten borrower
    B. Sell property without court order
    C. Initiate judicial foreclosure
    D. Evict the borrower

10. Which association represents title insurance?

    A. American Land Title Association
    B. CERCLA
    C. Fair Housing Act
    D. FEMA

11. Which law was passed to regulate credit bureaus?

    A. Annuity law
    B. Consumer credit law
    C. Fair Credit Reporting Act
    D. Truth in Lending Act

12. What is the legal right granted to exit a property?

    A. Easement
    B. Escheat
    C. Right of egress
    D. Right of ingress

13. What is the name given to non-monetary investment?

    A. Sweat equity
    B. Investment
    C. Capital
    D. Maintenance

14. What type of arrangement allows a borrower to negotiate a lower interest rate?

    A. Buydown
    B. Mortgage
    C. Purchase money
    D. Purchase price

15. What is a title without any lien?

    A. Clear title
    B. Deed
    C. Freehold
    D. Regular title

16. What is the name given to the breakdown of an individual's credit history?

    A. Credit assessment
    B. Credit report
    C. Financial record
    D. Repayment report

**17.** What is another term used to describe ownership?

   A.   Credit
   B.   Equity
   C.   Liability
   D.   Shares

**18.** What is the notice filed against a borrower on missing the repayment deadline?

   A.   Notice of cessation
   B.   Notice to cure
   C.   Notice of default
   D.   Notice of intention

**19.** What is the name given to describe the period a lender must keep a loan offer open to the borrower?

   A.   Due diligence period
   B.   Loan repayment period
   C.   Lock-in period
   D.   Target hold period

**20.** Which of the following is a lease break?

   A.   When a tenant breaks a rent prior to the date of expiry without a legal reason
   B.   When a tenant terminates a contract once the lease has expired
   C.   When a tenant breaks a lease with the agreement of the landlord
   D.   When a landlord allows a tenant to sublease his residence

**21.** What is the term used to refer to a situation where the amount of funds required to meet an obligation are **not** available?

   A.   Buydown
   B.   Debt to income ratio
   C.   Escrow
   D.   Shortfall

**22.** What is the term used to describe a situation where taxes are reduced or completely scrapped to increase buyers in the market?

   A.   Tax abatement
   B.   Tax exemption
   C.   Tax evasion
   D.   Duty free

**23.** A property originally assessed at $500,000 appreciated at 4% the first year and then 5% the year after. What is its current value?

   A.   $525,000
   B.   $545,000
   C.   $546,000
   D.   None of the above

**24.** Which entity performs the percolation test?

   A.   Department of State
   B.   Building Inspector
   C.   Homeowners Association
   D.   Department of Health

**25.** If a property is taxed at 25% with a tax levy of $92,000, what is its assessed value?

    A.   $65,000
    B.   $115,000
    C.   $122,666
    D.   $368,000

**26.** What is the name given to a brief summary of the history of a title?

    A.   Abstract of title
    B.   Chain of title
    C.   Deed chain
    D.   History of deed

**27.** What material is used in construction to cover joints where two or more types of materials meet?

    A.   Flashing
    B.   Metal
    C.   Wood
    D.   Joint

**28.** What is the lowest section of the roof that overhangs beyond the sidewalls of the building?

    A.   Eaves
    B.   Joists
    C.   Stud
    D.   Shingles

**29.** Which real estate metric is found by dividing cash flow by the deposit and settlement costs?

    A.   Cash out
    B.   Cash on cash return
    C.   Lock in period
    D.   Loan to value ratio

**30.** Which board committee is responsible for maintaining the aesthetic view of a town?

    A.   Architectural Review Board
    B.   Federal government
    C.   Municipality
    D.   HOA

**31.** What type of lease is taken on a loft?

    A.   Net lease
    B.   Gross lease
    C.   Percentage lease
    D.   Proprietary lease

**32.** What clause can prohibit having loud parties?

    A.   House rules
    B.   Regulations
    C.   Lease terms
    D.   Noise permit

**33.** What is the measurement used to show the volatility of a market?

  A. Fluctuation rate
  B. Absorption rate
  C. Inflation
  D. Purchase deviation

**34.** What is the mortgage clause that allows a lender the right to demand immediate payment of a mortgage?

  A. Cancellation clause
  B. Acceleration clause
  C. Prepayment Penalty clause
  D. Release clause

**35.** Which agreement allows a property holder to cross another person's land?

  A. Easement appurtenant
  B. Easement in gross
  C. Prescriptive easement
  D. None of the above

**36.** Which of the following is insurance taken out as a protection against malfunctions associated with the acquisition of a new home?

  A. Flood insurance
  B. Homeowner's warranty insurance
  C. HO2
  D. Hazard insurance

**37.** What is it called when someone takes possession of a property without being the actual title holder?

  A. Acceleration clause
  B. Adverse possession
  C. Easement
  D. Escheat

**38.** What is a non-possessory interest in property or restrictive covenant burdening the title?

  A. Adverse possession
  B. Easement
  C. Encumbrance
  D. Escheat

**39.** What is the name given to the long beams that span the piers of a foundation offering support to the floor or ceiling?

  A. Eaves
  B. Frames
  C. Joists
  D. Studs

**40.** What conveys a grantor's interest in real property?

  A. Agreement
  B. Conveyance
  C. Offering the loan
  D. Title

**41.** What prohibits the solicitation of residential property listings?

- A. Commingling
- B. Non-solicitation order
- C. Regulation Z
- D. Termination of tenancy

**42.** What is exempt from property taxation?

- A. Colleges
- B. Office buildings
- C. Supermarkets
- D. Unoccupied land

**43.** Which fiduciary duty is violated by commingling?

- A. Accountability
- B. Disclosure
- C. Obedience
- D. Loyalty

**44.** What gives the government power to appropriate private property?

- A. Right of first refusal
- B. Riparian rights
- C. Eminent domain
- D. None of the above

**45.** What is the owner of a building prohibited to do regarding the disabled?

- A. Allow the disabled to be tenants
- B. Make the building accessible to the disabled
- C. Ensure they are treated like other tenants
- D. Refuse modifications for handicapped tenants

**46.** What act prohibits discrimination based on disability?

- A. The Americans with Disabilities Act of 1990
- B. Fair Housing Act
- C. Civil Rights Act of 1866
- D. Civil Right Act of 1964

**47.** What is the name given to a property tenure that can be terminated at any time?

- A. Tenancy in sufferance
- B. Terminated tenancy
- C. Tenancy in common
- D. Tenancy at will

**48.** If you have a loan of $350,000 with a 7% interest, how much do you pay in interest every month?

- A. $2,041
- B. $2,260
- C. $27,125
- D. $31,208

**49.** What law prohibits any type of discrimination on the basis of sex and gender?

    A.   Fair Housing Act
    B.   Civil Rights Act of 1866
    C.   Civil Rights Act Amendment of 1974
    D.   Americans with Disabilities Act

**50.** In 1988, the Civil Rights Act was amended to include?

    A.   Married women
    B.   Immigrants
    C.   Black people
    D.   Handicaps and familial status

**51.** What is the net income of a property valued at $500,000 and a capitalization rate of 14%?

    A.   $70,000
    B.   $43,000
    C.   $840,000
    D.   None of the above

**52.** What is the name of an appointed official who estimates the value of real property for taxing purposes?

    A.   Agent
    B.   Assessor
    C.   Appraiser
    D.   Tax official

**53.** What is the term used to describe a situation where a mortgage balance decreases due to periodic installments that pay down the principal and interest?

    A.   Adjustable-rate mortgage
    B.   Amortization
    C.   Lock-in period
    D.   Fixed-rate mortgage

**54.** What is an annual tax levied on the value of real property?

    A.   Capital gains tax
    B.   Real estate tax
    C.   Progressive tax
    D.   Regressive tax

**55.** What is the name given to a situation where an individual uses borrowed money to purchase a property?

    A.   Buydown
    B.   Purchase money
    C.   Leverage
    D.   Shorting

**56.** Which air conditioning system facilitates both heating and cooling?

    A.   Forced air system
    B.   Cooling system
    C.   Heating system
    D.   Thermostat

**57.** What is the waiting time for a real estate agent to renew a license once it is revoked?

  A.  Two months
  B.  One year
  C.  Five years
  D.  It is never reinstated

**58.** Who manages a co-op?

  A.  Board of directors
  B.  CEO
  C.  Co-op developers
  D.  Tenants

**59.** What is the value estimating process that uses similar available properties to determine the value of land?

  A.  Mirror method
  B.  Sales comparison method
  C.  Allocation method
  D.  Abstraction method

**60.** Who is required to sign a deed in a real estate transaction?

  A.  Attorney
  B.  Buyer
  C.  Grantor
  D.  Lender

**61.** What is a poisonous gas that comes from the breakdown of minerals in soil?

  A.  Ammonia
  B.  Chlorine
  C.  Helium
  D.  Radon

**62.** What are the rights of a person whose property is adjacent to or crossed by a river?

  A.  Exclusive rights to sell
  B.  Riparian rights
  C.  Rights of first refusal
  D.  Right of disclosure

**63.** What law requires full disclosure of all credit terms for consumer loans under the Truth in Lending Act?

  A.  Americans with Disabilities Act
  B.  Civil Rights Act
  C.  Fair Housing Act
  D.  Regulation Z

**64.** What is the name given to granting priority to an individual to buy or lease a property?

  A.  Bundle of rights
  B.  Exclusive right to sell
  C.  Right of first refusal
  D.  Right of possession

Practice Tes

**65.** What is the loss of property value caused by economic or functional factors?

    A.    Economic obsolescence
    B.    Depreciation
    C.    Legal obsolescence
    D.    Aesthetic obsolescence

**66.** What kind of agent is a real estate agent?

    A.    Special agent
    B.    General agent
    C.    Dual agent
    D.    Subagent

**67.** What valuing method is Comparative Market Analysis **not** considered as?

    A.    Appraisal
    B.    Home valuing
    C.    Depreciation valuing
    D.    Tax returns valuing

**68.** What is a specific lien claimed by someone who has performed construction / repair / renovation work on the property and has **not** been paid?

    A.    Mechanic's lien
    B.    Involuntary lien
    C.    Mortgage
    D.    Judicial lien

**69.** What is the bottom piece of a frame that provides a nailing surface for the floor and wall system?

    A.    Eaves
    B.    Joist
    C.    Sill plate
    D.    Stud

**70.** What is a broker allowed to purchase for a real estate salesperson?

    A.    Phone
    B.    Medical insurance cover
    C.    Retirement plan
    D.    A company vehicle

**71.** When does a real estate salesperson first provide the agency disclosure form?

    A.    When the deal is about to be closed
    B.    After closing the deal
    C.    First substantial contact
    D.    Never

**72.** What is the definition of steering?

    A.    When you knowingly provide inaccurate information
    B.    The practice of guiding people away from certain homes based on factors such as race, religion or familial status
    C.    Discriminating against people due to socio-economic status
    D.    Failing to provide proof of continuing real estate education

**73.** What is the value of a point on a mortgage?

   A. 1% of loan
   B. 5% of the loan
   C. 10% of the loan
   D. 50% of the loan

**74.** What type of talent are real estate salespeople?

   A. Assistants
   B. Independent contractors
   C. Part time employees
   D. Full time employees

**75.** What is the term used to describe a building that is separate from the main house?

   A. Supplemental structure
   B. Accessory building
   C. Secondary land
   D. Shed

**76.** The estate that provides absolute ownership of land is called?

   A. Fee simple estate
   B. Life estate
   C. Conditional fee estate
   D. Legal life estate

**77.** Which of the following is an example of community property?

   A. Property that is inherited by the husband through marriage
   B. Income that is earned by one spouse during the marriage
   C. Income earned prior to marriage
   D. A gift given to one spouse during the marriage

**78.** Fixture are considered _____.

   A. Hypothecation
   B. An agreement between the two parties
   C. Items that are removable by the tenant before the expiration date of the lease
   D. Real property

**79.** The commission that is due to a salesperson is decided by?

   A. Chattels
   B. State Law
   C. Mutual Agreement
   D. Court Decree

**80.** A real estate broker has become an agent of the seller when _____.

   A. A listing agreement with the seller has been executed
   B. They are responsible for sharing commissions
   C. A broker acts in good faith
   D. They are procuring cause

**THIS IS THE END OF THE NATIONAL PORTION.**

## State Portion

1.  In Michigan broker and salespersons license expires every _____.

    A.  Year
    B.  3 years
    C.  2 years
    D.  4 years

2.  A broker has _____ to deliver a terminated salesperson's license to LARA.

    A.  3 months
    B.  1 month
    C.  5 days
    D.  24 hours

3.  Which of the following is not a violation of the occupational code in Michigan?

    A.  Failing to comply with a subpoena
    B.  Practicing real estate without a license
    C.  Changing brokerage locations without notifying the department
    D.  Practicing real estate in an adjoining county

4.  A broker's license has been revoked. How long must the broker wait to apply for a new license?

    A.  3 years
    B.  2 years
    C.  It varies for each case
    D.  5 years

**5.** Which of the following statements is true about brokerages in the state of Michigan?

    A.  An office can be either physical or virtual

    B.  A broker must maintain a physical office within the state

    C.  There can only be 5 brokers per office

    D.  None of the above

**6.** Which statement is true about commission in the state of Michigan?

    A.  Commission cannot exceed 20% of property value

    B.  A salesperson can only receive commission from the employing broker

    C.  A salesperson cannot receive commission

    D.  All of the above is true

**7.** Which of the following statements is not true about real estate advertisements in the state of Michigan?

    A.  Advertisements must indicate that they are the broker

    B.  Advertisement must include a broker's name

    C.  Blind ads are legal in the state of Michigan

    D.  None of the above is true

**8.** Which type of listing is illegal in Michigan?

    A.  Exclusive agency listing

    B.  Option listing

    C.  Exclusive right to sell

    D.  Net listing

**9.** In co-brokering, who is responsible for closing the sale and furnishing the signed closing statements to the buyer and seller?

    A. Buyer's agent
    B. Listing broker
    C. Either broker
    D. Broker with the most experience

**10.** What is the seller disclosure statement?

    A. A document, required by the state, that discloses certain information about the property's physical condition
    B. A document completed by an appraiser prior to a sale
    C. A list of demands from the buyer to complete the sale of a home
    D. None of the above

**11.** How many days does the broker have to deposit money into an escrow account?

    A. 5 banking days
    B. 3 banking days
    C. 2 banking days
    D. 1 banking day

**12.** In Michigan, all real estate contracts must be in writing except for _____.

    A. A lease that is a year or less in length
    B. When property is being sold to a family member
    C. When a real estate transaction is in cash
    D. All of the above

**13.** According to the Michigan's Home Solicitation Sales Act, consumers have _____ to cancel a contract in the case of solicitation.

    A.   5 days
    B.   3 days
    C.   10 days
    D.   7 days

**14.** Michigan law requires that all licensees _____.

    A.   Explain the different client relationships that can exist prior to disclosing confidential information
    B.   Have clients sign agency disclosure before signing other documents
    C.   Present the client agency disclosure to all possible clients at the earliest possible time
    D.   All of the above

**15.** A pending contract is also called a(n) _____.

    A.   Executed
    B.   Arbitration
    C.   Blockbusting
    D.   Executory

**16.** A _____ is also referred to as an installment sale agreement or contract for deed.

    A.   Equitable title
    B.   Land contract
    C.   Commingling
    D.   Tort

**17.** When one party is replaced with another party in a contract it is called a _____.

   A. Novation
   B. Cessation
   C. Transfer
   D. None of the above

**18.** Which statement is true about real estate deposits in the state of Michigan?

   A. The salesperson has the ability to accept and deposit checks into the escrow account
   B. The salesperson cannot accept checks made out to them personally
   C. The salesperson cannot accept any checks from a principal
   D. All of the above are true

**19.** Which of the following is not a type of service provision agreement?

   A. A listing agreement
   B. Land contract
   C. Buyer agency agreement
   D. All of the above are types of service provision agreement

**20.** Which of the following is illegal when renting or leasing property?

   A. Denying a dwelling due to their sex
   B. Set different terms, conditions or privileges based on a person's race
   C. Provide different housing services or facilities based on a person's religion
   D. All of the above

21. This Michigan state law prohibits discrimination in any activity related to the sale or rental of dwellings, financing, or insuring housing.

   A. Discrimination Act
   B. Housing and Urban Development Act
   C. Fair Housing Laws
   D. Non-discrimination Act

22. Which of the following is not a requirement to become a property manager in Michigan?

   A. 3 years full-time experience in real estate
   B. 90 hours of approved broker level education
   C. Pass an examination
   D. 90 hours of approved salesperson level education

23. There is only one reason when the landlord may immediately remove a tenant from the premises. Which of the following is that reason?

   A. If the tenant refuses to pay rent
   B. If the tenant gets in trouble with the law
   C. If the tenant violates the terms of the lease
   D. If the local authorities deem the premises unfit for occupancy

24. Licensing and Regulatory Affair (LARA) has 15 days to _____.

   A. Acknowledge the sale of a brokerage
   B. Acknowledge the receipt of a complaint to a complainant
   C. Respond to a compliant from a consumer
   D. Respond to a complaint from a licensee

Practice Tes

**25.** The simultaneous ownership of real property by two or more people is called a _____.

    A. Concurrent ownership
    B. Multi tenancy
    C. Dower estate
    D. None of the above

**26.** Which of the following is not a Michigan law that affects landlords and property managers?

    A. Michigan Property Law
    B. Truth in Renting
    C. Landlord Tenant Relationship Act
    D. Summary Procedures Act

**27.** This state law defines and regulates home improvement charge agreements and home improvement installment contracts in Michigan.

    A. Home Improvement Finance Act
    B. Truth in Renting
    C. Michigan Property Law
    D. None of the above

**28.** According to the Michigan Condominium Act, a new condominium construction agreement is binding 9 days after the developer delivers which of the following documents to the purchaser?

    A. The recorded master deed with the attached bylaws and sub plans
    B. A copy of the purchase and escrow agreements
    C. The condominium buyer's handbook
    D. All of the above

29. The _____ receives, investigates, and holds hearings on complaints regarding unfair housing practices.

   A. Michigan Civil Rights Commission
   B. Department of Licensing and Regulatory Affairs
   C. Associate of Real Estate Licensing Laws
   D. District courts

30. A landlord shuts off the heating and lights making the property unlivable. The tenant decides to leave the property, this is called _____.

   A. Actual eviction
   B. Quit notice
   C. Constructive eviction
   D. None of the above

31. Which of the following state laws prohibits illegal clauses and unlawful discrimination?

   A. Security Deposit Act
   B. Truth in Renting
   C. Summary Procedures Act
   D. None of the above

32. Which statement is true about the Michigan Landlord Tenant Relationship Act?

   A. A landlord can only require 1.5 times a month's rent as a security deposit
   B. This act only applies to commercial leases
   C. This act applies to both commercial and residential leases
   D. A&C only

**33.** Which of the following laws prohibits discrimination?

A. Civil Rights Act
B. Non-discrimination Act
C. Fair Housing Act
D. Citizen's Rights Act

**34.** Which of the following statements is true about real estate licensees in Michigan?

A. A licensee cannot host an open house
B. The licensee cannot provide legal advice to the principal
C. The licensee cannot accept commission from family members
D. All of the above is true

**35.** Which law provides the detailed rights of a purchaser or prospective purchaser of a condominium in the state?

A. Federal Condominium Act
B. Michigan Condominium Act
C. Michigan Buyer Act
D. Condominium Act of Michigan

**THIS IS THE END OF THE STATE PORTION.**

# Answer Key – National Portion

| | | | | | | | |
|---|---|---|---|---|---|---|---|
| 1. | C | 21. | D | 41. | B | 61. | D |
| 2. | A | 22. | A | 42. | A | 62. | B |
| 3. | D | 23. | C | 43. | A | 63. | D |
| 4. | A | 24. | D | 44. | C | 64. | C |
| 5. | C | 25. | D | 45. | D | 65. | A |
| 6. | B | 26. | A | 46. | A | 66. | A |
| 7. | D | 27. | A | 47. | D | 67. | A |
| 8. | C | 28. | A | 48. | A | 68. | A |
| 9. | C | 29. | B | 49. | C | 69. | C |
| 10. | A | 30. | A | 50. | D | 70. | A |
| 11. | C | 31. | B | 51. | A | 71. | C |
| 12. | C | 32. | A | 52. | B | 72. | B |
| 13. | A | 33. | B | 53. | B | 73. | A |
| 14. | A | 34. | B | 54. | B | 74. | B |
| 15. | A | 35. | A | 55. | C | 75. | B |
| 16. | B | 36. | B | 56. | A | 76. | A |
| 17. | B | 37. | B | 57. | B | 77. | B |
| 18. | C | 38. | C | 58. | A | 78. | D |
| 19. | C | 39. | C | 59. | D | 79. | C |
| 20. | A | 40. | B | 60. | C | 80. | A |

1.      **C) Foreclosure**

This is the legal process where a lender seeks to recover the balance of a loan by selling the property held as collateral. Foreclosure usually occurs after a lender has legally obtained a termination of the borrower's right of redemption.

2.      **A) Asbestos**

Asbestos is a naturally occurring mineral and its insulation qualities make it popular in making fireproof materials. When products containing asbestos are disturbed, they release tiny fibers in the air that when inhaled over a long period of time can be detrimental as they accumulate in the lung causing scarring and inflammation. Continued exposure affects cells resulting in a rare cancer known as mesothelioma.

3.      **D) Studs**

These are vertical beams that are used during construction to frame the house. They are used to form or position walls in a building. Previously, studs made of timber dominated the construction industry but modern construction styles have embraced the use of steel.

4.  **A) Misrepresentation**

Misrepresentation occurs when a broker misstates information of property. It is a false statement that may affect a person's decision to enter into a contract. Three types of misrepresentation are fraudulent misrepresentation, negligent misrepresentation and innocent misrepresentation.

5.  **C) Preventive maintenance**

In order to maintain tenants and an acceptable return on an investment, routine checks and repairs have to be done. These are done to safeguard against failing which may incur losses to the property manager that arise due to cost of replacement.

6.  **B) Mortgagee**

A mortgagee is an entity that lends money for the purpose of buying a real estate property. As a precaution, the mortgagee establishes prior interest in the property and maintains the title as collateral.

7.  **D) $156,250**

$150,000 / (1 - 0.04) = $156,250

8.  **C) Land zoning**

This refers to the restriction of physical development and the use of certain parcels of land. It is done with regard to zoning laws and purposes to protect wildlife and natural resources. It is also used to restrict the number of domestic animals that can be accommodated on a property.

9.  **C) Initiate judicial foreclosure**

Judicial foreclosure are court proceedings that allow the lender to seize the property that was held as collateral for sale. This is done in order to regain the principal amount. This can only be done once it has been established that a defaulting borrower is unable to continue making payments.

10. **A) American Land Title Association**

This is a trade association that is aimed at trying to improve oversight by representing title insurance.

11.     **C) Fair Credit Reporting Act**

Credit reporting is the process of collecting and analyzing consumers credit information by credit bureaus. This information is sold to lending facilities in order to help them determine whether or not a borrower is eligible for a loan. This act was passed to highlight consumer rights when it comes to credit information.

12.     **C) Right of egress**

This is the legal right granted to homeowners as they allow access to property. These rights are usually obtained through an easement and apply regardless of the property type.

13.     **A) Sweat equity**

This is the non-monetary equity that owners contribute into the business or property. In this case, sweat equity is the amount of effort an owner puts into a property in order to increase its value.

14.     **A) Buydown**

This is a mortgage-financing technique that allows a borrower to negotiate lower monthly payment rates. It usually involves the seller making payments to the lending institution to reduce monthly payment rate of the buyer. As a result, the purchase price goes up.

15.     **A) Clear title**

A clear title is a title that has no liens or levies from creditors and other involved parties. A clear title is used to ensure there is no question of ownership. It shows that there are no outstanding financial responsibilities attached to the property and the owner is legally capable of selling the property.

16.     **B) Credit report**

A credit report is a detailed breakdown of an individual's credit history and is usually carried out by credit bureaus. They use financial information attached to an individual like their bill payment to establish a unique report. This information is usually used by lenders while considering a loan applicant.

17.     **B) Equity**

Equity is another term for ownership. In home investments, equity means the amount of principal that has been paid off. The higher the equity the easier it is to refinance a property.

18. **C) Notice of default**

This is a public notice filed in court regarding a borrower's default on a loan. It is usually to notify the borrower that there has been a breach in the contractual limit that had been predetermined in the loan. A grace period is included for negotiation before further action is considered.

19. **C) Lock-in period**

This is the period usually 30 to 60 days within which a lender is required to keep a loan offer open. This gives the borrower enough time to prepare for closing while the lender is processing the loan. A lock in period protects the borrower from losses incurred throughout the repayment of the loan caused by rising interest rates during processing of the loan.

20. **A) When a tenant breaks a rent prior to the date of expiry without a legal reason**

As a lease is a contract, breaking a lease without a valid reason may result in being sued by the landlord. To avoid legal action, the individual breaking the lease must prove beyond reasonable doubt that the break was caused by a situation completely out of their hands.

21. **D) Shortfall**

Shortfall is a term used to describe a situation where a financial obligation exceeds the required amount of cash available. A shortfall may be a temporary and current situation or a prolonged one. The latter represents mismanagement of funds and warrants a deeper look into spending habits and change has to be implemented.

22. **A) Tax abatement**

Tax abatement is a strategy used by the government to increase investments in specific areas. In the real estate sector, tax abatement occurs when taxes on properties are significantly reduced or completely eliminated. It is usually done to encourage investors to buy property in areas that have recorded long term low demand.

23. **C) $546,000**

$500,000 * 1.04 * 1.05 = $546,000

24. **D) Department of Health**

A percolation test (also known as a perc test) is a soil evaluation performed during a vacant land or septic permit site evaluation. A representative from the local department of health determines if an applicant's property will allow for the installation of a sewage system.

25. **D) $368,000**

$92,000 / 0.25 = $368,000

26.    **A) Abstract of title**

This is a summarized history of all title transfers and legal actions that have been connected with a certain property. It is beneficial in preventing home buyers from getting tangled in legal issues that are attached to a property. This is because any loss made because of a court ruling on a property once a buyer has purchased will be incurred by the new tenant.

27.    **A) Flashing**

This is a material used to cover joints where two or more types of material join. This usually happens to prevent water leakage through the joint. It also provides a drainage between two joints.

28.    **A) Eaves**

This is a part of the roof that projects over the wall beyond the edge of the roof. It is usually set in place to channel water away from the roof.

29.    **B) Cash on cash return**

Cash on cash return that a proven metric used to calculate future cash returns on a cash investment. This metric is only true for a cash investment and does not take into account loan investments.

30.    **A) Architectural Review Board**

The Architectural Review Board is given the responsibility of upholding the visual integrity of a town. It is responsible for reviewing all exterior designs of all residential and commercial structures in a town. All new structures and structures that are up for alteration are required to provide a blueprint of the exterior design for printing. They are also charged with ensuring commercial signs conform to the towns design.

31.    **B) Gross lease**

A gross lease is a lease where a flat rent fee is paid. It includes rent and other utility fees such as taxes and insurance. A landlord is obligated to calculate a rate based on history or research. A negotiation between the tenant and landlord can also be reached on the services the tenant wants to be included in the lease.

32.    **A) House rules**

These are rules that are given to tenants of a coop or condo on the beginning of the contract regarding behavior within the complex. They are put in place to ensure a comfortable living space for all occupants. Failure to adhere to the rules may result in eviction.

33. **B) Absorption rate**

This is a ration of the number of properties that have been sold against the number of properties that are available for sale within a specified area.

34. **B) Acceleration clause**

This is a provision in a mortgage that allows the lender the right to demand the immediate settlement on a mortgage under certain predetermined conditions such as a borrower defaulting on a loan.

35. **A) Easement appurtenant**

Easement appurtenant is an agreement that is transferable with ownership rights of a property. When a property is transferred through sale or inheritance, all rights and privileges attached to the land are automatically transferred to the new owner.

36. **B) Homeowner's warranty insurance**

Homeowner's warranty insurance insures the homeowner from the builder's faults for a specified warranty period

37. **B) Adverse possession**

This is a legal principle that allows a person who has been living on a specific land for a long period of time to take possession of the land without permission of the owner. The individual does not have to have a title to the land to acquire it. The title holder is capable of claiming his land by choosing to eject the squatter.

38. **C) Encumbrance**

This is a limitation against a real estate property. It restricts the owner from transferring ownership of the title. It also prevents an owner from depreciating the value of the property.

39. **C) Joists**

These are horizontal structural members used to frame an open space. They are often used in transferring loads to the vertical members of the structure. When used in floors, they provide stiffness in the framing systems.

40. **B) Conveyance**

A conveyance or sale deed is a legally binding contract that transfers all ownership rights from the seller to the buyer. It usually states the agreed-on price, the date of the transaction and the obligations of the parties involved.

41. **B) Non-solicitation order**

This is an order issued to broker and agents to prevent them from soliciting listings in designated areas

42. **A) Colleges**

Despite the fact that all property is assessed to determine its value, universities, schools, parks, government institutions, religious organizations, and hospitals are exempt from property taxes. Veterans are also eligible from partial exemption from taxes.

43. **A) Accountability**

Commingling is a contract breach where a fiduciary mixed funds belonging to a client with his own making it impossible to separate them. The accountability clause requires a fiduciary to be able to maintain an accurate report of documents and funds that he/she has been entrusted.

44. **C) Eminent domain**

This is the government's power to take private land for public use under certain circumstances. It is defined by the Taking Clause of the Fifth Amendment which prohibits the taking of private land without just compensation. It emphasizes that the government can only take land for public use and offer just compensation on the land.

45. **D) Refuse modifications for handicapped tenants**

Refuse to allow tenants to make reasonable structural modifications to a unit at the tenant's expense to allow the handicapped tenant full enjoyment of the property (Fair Housing Act). In accordance with the Fair Housing Act which is against discrimination in housing, multifamily buildings are expected to ensure accessibility for people using wheelchairs

46. **A) The Americans with Disabilities Act of 1990**

This act was enacted to ensure disabled people are not discriminated against and have equal rights regarding access to employment and commercial facilities.

47. **D) Tenancy at will**

This is a tenancy that is not bound by a lease and does not have an expiry or duration of tenancy. A predetermined payment plan is adhered and a tenant is flexible to terminate the tenancy without legal proceedings. It is a beneficial plan for landlords and tenants that seek flexibility.

48. **A) $2,041**

($350,000 * 0.07) / 12 = $2,041

**49.** **C) Civil Rights Act Amendment of 1974**

The Civil Rights act amendment of 1974 banned discrimination based on sex and credit in a congress proceeding. Women being offered maternity leave on the assumption that they were unable to work was rendered illegal and sexist teaching methods were discredited.

**50.** **D) Handicaps and familial status**

The act protects people with disabilities and families with children. Pregnant women were also protected from illegal discrimination.

**51.** **A) $70,000**

$500,000 * 0.14 = $70,000

**52.** **B) Assessor**

An assessor is a government official that is engaged to determine the value of a property. The information gathered by an assessor is used to calculate future property taxes. Assessors maintain annual assessments at a uniform percentage of market value.

**53.** **B) Amortization**

This is the scheduling of monthly mortgage payments showing breakdown of payment. When paying a mortgage loan for a property, the initial payments are put towards paying off the interest and less is allocated to the principal amount. As a borrower makes more payments, more is allocated to the principal and less to the interest.

**54.** **B) Real estate tax**

This is an ad valorem tax on the value of a property. It is levied annually on real estate by the government authority.

**55.** **C) Leverage**

This refers to money that has been borrowed to finance an investment property. The leverage concept works best when rent and property values are on the rise. Monthly mortgage payments for the rental property become constant which results in a rise in profits

**56.** **A) Forced air system**

A forced air system refers to any HVAC system that makes use of air ducts and vents to release temperature-controlled air into the building. A forced air system released filtered and dehumidified cold air into buildings and runs at an affordable price. A central air system on the other hand uses vents in the forced air system to provide cool and conditioned air.

57.     **B) One year**

An individual is required to wait for an entire year after which the agent is required to prove with evidence that he/she is capable of being trustworthy and upholding the law with regard to the real estate sector.

58.     **A) Board of directors**

A co-op is an alternative method to traditional housing. A board of directors is elected by the shareholders to run the corporation. They are responsible for vetting and doing background checks on potential new shareholders in the corporation. They are also responsible for upholding the values and regulations of the co-op and terminating tenancy of individuals found to be acting contrary to the rules.

59.     **D) Abstraction method**

This is a method of estimating the value of a piece of land that is based on the going price of similar parcels of land within the area.

60.     **C) Grantor**

This is the party that transfers ownership of property to buyer through a legal document known as a deed. The grantor is required to sign the deed admitting the transfer of ownership before closing. The deed is then filed at the county jurisdiction for public record.

61.     **D) Radon**

Radon is a radioactive cancer-causing gas that comes from the natural breakdown of uranium in soil. The gas penetrates its way into houses from cracks and holes in the foundation. Testing for radon gas is mandatory during purchasing of a home in order to fix the problem by lowering the amount of radon gas available to the acceptable amounts.

62.     **B) Riparian rights**

These are rights that arise when an individual owns land near a moving watercourse. These rights include swimming and irrigation. The rights only attach when there's a water on one side of the land. An individual is allowed to benefit from the water body without contaminating or altering the flow of the waterbody.

63.     **D) Regulation Z**

It requires lenders to make comprehensive disclosure statements to borrowers for consumer loans. It is aimed at protecting consumers from misleading lending practices. Lenders are required to disclose interest rates, finance charges, explain terms used and respond to all complaints launched by the borrower. This law was passed to ensure that borrowers make informed credit choices.

 81

64. **C) Right of first refusal**

This is the right given to a specific party to purchase or lease a property before it is open to bidding by other potential buyers. The party being offered the privilege is not obligated to buy the property. In the event that the party is not interested in the property, it is opened up to the public.

65. **A) Economic obsolescence**

This is the decrease in the market value of a property due to external factors that cannot be controlled by the property owner i.e. building of an interstate highway close to a prime property. Its value immediately decreases due to the noise pollution.

66. **A) Special agent**

A special agent is an agent whose services are only employed for a specific task. Once the task is completed a special agent no longer has authority to represent the client.

67. **A) Appraisal**

An appraisal in a professional opinion value assessment of a property and is independent of the market values of similar properties based on the fact that all properties are unique and cannot be compared to each other.

68. **A) Mechanic's lien**

This is a security interest in title of property for the benefit of those who supplied materials and offered professional services on the construction and renovation of a property. A mechanic's lien can be taken on both real and personal properties.

69. **C) Sill plate**

This is a horizontal member of a wall where vertical members of the building are attached. It usually lies between the foundation and floor frame.

70. **A) Phone**

This is because salespeople are considered independent contractors and therefore are not eligible for company benefits.

71. **C) First substantial contact**

This refers to the earliest practicable opportunity during a conversation with the consumer. An agency disclosure is to be provided to disclose and explain the nature of the representation in a real estate transaction.

72. **B) The practice of guiding people away from certain homes based on factors such as race, religion or familial status**

Steering is an unlawful practice that violates the federal fair housing provisions. It is a practice in which brokers influence the choice of a prospective buyer or tenant based on race, religion, or familiar status.

73. **A) 1% of loan**

A value point is a fee paid directly to the lender at closing in exchange for a reduced interest rate and can lower a borrower's monthly mortgage payment.

74. **B) Independent contractors**

Independent contractors are hired to perform a service but are not included in the employee catalogue. Their main goal is to complete the task and the employing broker has no control over the process of yielding results or financial expenses incurred.

75. **B) Accessory building**

This is a building that is built separately from the main structure in a property. It is usually put to use for a specific purpose such as a shed, workshop or garage.

76. **A) Fee simple estate**

This provides absolute ownership of the land and allows the owner to do whatever they choose to with the land. This is the highest form of ownership in real estate.

77. **B) Income that is earned by one spouse during the marriage**

Community property is defined as everything that a married couple owns together. This includes income and property acquired during the duration of the marriage.

78. **D) Real property**

A fixture is physically property that is permanently attached to real property (on it or under it), that cannot be moved. Examples include ponds, canals, buildings and roads.

79. **C) Mutual Agreement**

An agreement between a buyer and a seller. It is a binding contract between the two parties and includes any contingencies.

80. **A) A listing agreement with the seller has been executed**

A listing agreement is a contract between the homeowner and a selling agent. It is a legal agreement that gives the selling agent the right to sell the home.

84

# Answer Key – State Portion

| | | | |
|---|---|---|---|
| 1. | B | 21. | C |
| 2. | C | 22. | D |
| 3. | D | 23. | D |
| 4. | A | 24. | B |
| 5. | B | 25. | A |
| 6. | B | 26. | A |
| 7. | C | 27. | A |
| 8. | D | 28. | D |
| 9. | B | 29. | A |
| 10. | A | 30. | C |
| 11. | C | 31. | B |
| 12. | A | 32. | A |
| 13. | B | 33. | A |
| 14. | D | 34. | B |
| 15. | D | 35. | B |
| 16. | B | | |
| 17. | A | | |
| 18. | B | | |
| 19. | B | | |
| 20. | D | | |

1. **B) 3 years**

   The licenses for both salespersons and brokers expire on the 31st of October every three years. There is 6 hours of continuing education for a total of 18 hours per three-year cycle.

2. **C) 5 days**

   The broker must be given written notice of termination and must send the salesperson's license to the department by certified mail.

3. **D) Practicing real estate in an adjoining county**

   The violations of the occupational code include practicing or committing fraud, false advertisement, incompetence, and failure to maintain escrow funds. Penalties will be enforced by the courts.

4. **A) 3 years**

   A broker or salesperson must wait 3 years to apply for a license after it has been revoked in the state of Michigan.

5. **B) A broker must maintain a physical office within the state**

Real estate businesses are required to have a physical office within the state of Michigan.

6. **B) A salesperson can only receive commission from the employing broker**

A salesperson can only receive commission and other compensations from employing broker.

7. **C) Blind ads are legal in the state of Michigan**

Blind ads are not legal in Michigan. That means an ad must have the broker's name and a phone number or post office box number.

8. **D) Net listing**

This type of listing allows the agent to keep any amount of money over the price set by the seller. This type of listing is illegal in Michigan.

9. **B) Listing broker**

Either broker has the right to close the sale and furnish closing statements but the final responsibility of the listing broker to close the sale and furnish signed closing statements to the buyer and seller.

10. **A) A document, required by the state, that discloses certain information about the property's physical condition**

This disclosure is required by the state of Michigan and must be provided to the seller prior to the completion of the sale. This disclosure will not relieve an agent of civil liability

11. **C) 2 banking days**

After the broker has received notice that an offer to purchase has been accepted by all parties, the broker has two banking days to deposit monies given for the sale.

12. **A) A lease that is a year or less in length**

A lease that is for a year or less does not have to be in writing. All other real estate contracts must be in writing to be valid.

13. **B) 3 days**

This law gives consumers 3 days to decide whether to cancel a contract if they were being solicited in their homes.

14. **D) All of the above**

All of the above is a requirement. This information is also required to be in writing for it to be valid.

15. **D) Executory**

This type of contract is one that is pending and has not been executed. This may take effect on a future contingency. A contract that has been performed is an executed contract.

16. **B) Land contract**

At closing the buyer agrees to pay a specified amount of money to the seller for a certain period of time and at the end of the payments the seller agrees to give the buyer the deed for the property. The buyer has equitable title and the seller retains legal title.

17. **A) Novation**

This is a contract that substitutes one party in a preexisting contract with another party who was not originally apart of the contract.

18. **B) The salesperson cannot accept checks made out to them personally**

A salesperson who has received a deposit needs to give it to the employing broker immediately.

19. **B) Land contract**

A service provision contract is a contract that creates an agency relationship with a client.

20. **D) All of the above**

All of the above is illegal when leasing or renting property. Other things that are illegal are refusing to rent, falsely denying that housing is available, blockbusting, and denying access to or membership in a facility or service.

21. **C) Fair Housing Laws**

Michigan's Fair Housing Laws is made up of the Elliot-Larson Civil Rights Act and Persons with Disabilities Civil Rights Act.

22. **D) 90 hours of approved salesperson level education**

This is not true a licensee must have 90 hours of approved broker level education not salesperson education.

23.     **D) If the local authorities deem the premises unfit for occupancy**

This is also called condemnation. The landlord can exert the right to remove the tenant if the property has been deemed unfit.

24.     **B) Acknowledge the receipt of a complaint to a complainant**

LARA is responsible for addressing all real estate complaints and they are required to acknowledge the complaint within 15 days.

25.     **A) Concurrent ownership**

A concurrent ownership is property that can be owned by more than one person at a given time. It is also referred to as concurrent estate.

26.     **A) Michigan Property Law**

This is not a Michigan law. The rest of the laws are Michigan laws that affect landlord and property managers.

27.     **A) Home Improvement Finance Act**

This state law regulates contracts for the modernization, rehabilitation, repair, alteration, or improvement upon or in connection with real property. It also provides the functions of circuit courts, attorney generals, attorneys and provides remedies and penalties.

28.     **D) All of the above**

All of the above must be provided to the consumer to make the construction agreement binding. A disclosure statement is also required.

29.     **A) Michigan Civil Rights Commission**

This organization is responsible for the complaint process regarding unfair housing practices. The complaints must be made within 180 days after the alleged unfair housing practice occurred.

30.     **C) Constructive eviction**

This occurs when an activity makes it difficult for the tenant to live on the premises. Other examples are not making repairs that are needed and is illegal.

         Practice Tes

31.	**B) Truth in Renting**

This law prohibits illegal clauses and unlawful discrimination. It also requires the landlord to state their name and address, provide a paragraph about understanding the contract and regulates publishers of preprinted rental agreement forms.

32.	**A) A landlord can only require 1.5 times a month's rent as a security deposit**

This law applies to residential leases only and it states that any amount of money that has been collected outside of rent for the first rental period that is held for the duration of the lease becomes a part of the security deposit.

33.	**A) Civil Rights Act**

This act prohibits discrimination on the basis of race. There is no limit on punitive damages for violating this act.

34.	**B) The licensee cannot provide legal advice to the principal**

A licensee must refrain from providing legal advice. Only an attorney can provide legal advice.

35.	**B) Michigan Condominium Act**

This state law provides the detailed rights of a condominium purchaser. It states that the developer of a new construction condominium must provide prospective purchasers detailed information concerning the construction and proposed operating procedures.

# Practice Test 3

Directions:

1.      You have a 3-hour time limit to complete the whole exam.

2.      To pass, you must answer at least 70% of all questions correctly.

3.      Some questions will require mathematics. You may use a calculator.

4.      **Phones and pagers are not allowed. Having either will result in automatic dismissal from the exam and nullification of exam scores.**

Tips:

- Answer all questions even if you are unsure.
- Mark any questions you are stuck on and revisit them after you are done. The exam is timed so make sure you finish as many questions as you can.
- After reading the question, try answering it in your head first to avoid getting confused by the choices.
- Read the entire question before looking at the answers.
- Use the process of elimination to filter out choices that don't seem correct to increase your chances of selecting the correct answer.
- Be aware of important keywords like **not, sometimes, always,** and **never**. These words completely alter the ask of the question so it's important to keep track of them.

**PLEASE READ THESE INSTRUCTIONS CAREFULLY.**

# Practice Test 3

Name: _____　　　　　　　　　　　　　　Date: _____

## NATIONAL PORTION

| | | | | | | | | | | | | | | |
|---|---|---|---|---|---|---|---|---|---|---|---|---|---|---|
| 1. | Ⓐ Ⓑ Ⓒ Ⓓ | | 31. | Ⓐ Ⓑ Ⓒ Ⓓ | | 61. | Ⓐ Ⓑ Ⓒ Ⓓ |
| 2. | Ⓐ Ⓑ Ⓒ Ⓓ | | 32. | Ⓐ Ⓑ Ⓒ Ⓓ | | 62. | Ⓐ Ⓑ Ⓒ Ⓓ |
| 3. | Ⓐ Ⓑ Ⓒ Ⓓ | | 33. | Ⓐ Ⓑ Ⓒ Ⓓ | | 63. | Ⓐ Ⓑ Ⓒ Ⓓ |
| 4. | Ⓐ Ⓑ Ⓒ Ⓓ | | 34. | Ⓐ Ⓑ Ⓒ Ⓓ | | 64. | Ⓐ Ⓑ Ⓒ Ⓓ |
| 5. | Ⓐ Ⓑ Ⓒ Ⓓ | | 35. | Ⓐ Ⓑ Ⓒ Ⓓ | | 65. | Ⓐ Ⓑ Ⓒ Ⓓ |
| 6. | Ⓐ Ⓑ Ⓒ Ⓓ | | 36. | Ⓐ Ⓑ Ⓒ Ⓓ | | 66. | Ⓐ Ⓑ Ⓒ Ⓓ |
| 7. | Ⓐ Ⓑ Ⓒ Ⓓ | | 37. | Ⓐ Ⓑ Ⓒ Ⓓ | | 67. | Ⓐ Ⓑ Ⓒ Ⓓ |
| 8. | Ⓐ Ⓑ Ⓒ Ⓓ | | 38. | Ⓐ Ⓑ Ⓒ Ⓓ | | 68. | Ⓐ Ⓑ Ⓒ Ⓓ |
| 9. | Ⓐ Ⓑ Ⓒ Ⓓ | | 39. | Ⓐ Ⓑ Ⓒ Ⓓ | | 69. | Ⓐ Ⓑ Ⓒ Ⓓ |
| 10. | Ⓐ Ⓑ Ⓒ Ⓓ | | 40. | Ⓐ Ⓑ Ⓒ Ⓓ | | 70. | Ⓐ Ⓑ Ⓒ Ⓓ |
| 11. | Ⓐ Ⓑ Ⓒ Ⓓ | | 41. | Ⓐ Ⓑ Ⓒ Ⓓ | | 71. | Ⓐ Ⓑ Ⓒ Ⓓ |
| 12. | Ⓐ Ⓑ Ⓒ Ⓓ | | 42. | Ⓐ Ⓑ Ⓒ Ⓓ | | 72. | Ⓐ Ⓑ Ⓒ Ⓓ |
| 13. | Ⓐ Ⓑ Ⓒ Ⓓ | | 43. | Ⓐ Ⓑ Ⓒ Ⓓ | | 73. | Ⓐ Ⓑ Ⓒ Ⓓ |
| 14. | Ⓐ Ⓑ Ⓒ Ⓓ | | 44. | Ⓐ Ⓑ Ⓒ Ⓓ | | 74. | Ⓐ Ⓑ Ⓒ Ⓓ |
| 15. | Ⓐ Ⓑ Ⓒ Ⓓ | | 45. | Ⓐ Ⓑ Ⓒ Ⓓ | | 75. | Ⓐ Ⓑ Ⓒ Ⓓ |
| 16. | Ⓐ Ⓑ Ⓒ Ⓓ | | 46. | Ⓐ Ⓑ Ⓒ Ⓓ | | 76. | Ⓐ Ⓑ Ⓒ Ⓓ |
| 17 | Ⓐ Ⓑ Ⓒ Ⓓ | | 47. | Ⓐ Ⓑ Ⓒ Ⓓ | | 77. | Ⓐ Ⓑ Ⓒ Ⓓ |
| 18. | Ⓐ Ⓑ Ⓒ Ⓓ | | 48. | Ⓐ Ⓑ Ⓒ Ⓓ | | 78. | Ⓐ Ⓑ Ⓒ Ⓓ |
| 19. | Ⓐ Ⓑ Ⓒ Ⓓ | | 49. | Ⓐ Ⓑ Ⓒ Ⓓ | | 79. | Ⓐ Ⓑ Ⓒ Ⓓ |
| 20. | Ⓐ Ⓑ Ⓒ Ⓓ | | 50. | Ⓐ Ⓑ Ⓒ Ⓓ | | 80. | Ⓐ Ⓑ Ⓒ Ⓓ |
| 21. | Ⓐ Ⓑ Ⓒ Ⓓ | | 51. | Ⓐ Ⓑ Ⓒ Ⓓ | | | |
| 22. | Ⓐ Ⓑ Ⓒ Ⓓ | | 52. | Ⓐ Ⓑ Ⓒ Ⓓ | | | |
| 23. | Ⓐ Ⓑ Ⓒ Ⓓ | | 53. | Ⓐ Ⓑ Ⓒ Ⓓ | | | |
| 24. | Ⓐ Ⓑ Ⓒ Ⓓ | | 54. | Ⓐ Ⓑ Ⓒ Ⓓ | | | |
| 25. | Ⓐ Ⓑ Ⓒ Ⓓ | | 55. | Ⓐ Ⓑ Ⓒ Ⓓ | | | |
| 26. | Ⓐ Ⓑ Ⓒ Ⓓ | | 56. | Ⓐ Ⓑ Ⓒ Ⓓ | | | |
| 27. | Ⓐ Ⓑ Ⓒ Ⓓ | | 57. | Ⓐ Ⓑ Ⓒ Ⓓ | | | |
| 28. | Ⓐ Ⓑ Ⓒ Ⓓ | | 58. | Ⓐ Ⓑ Ⓒ Ⓓ | | | |
| 29. | Ⓐ Ⓑ Ⓒ Ⓓ | | 59. | Ⓐ Ⓑ Ⓒ Ⓓ | | | |
| 30. | Ⓐ Ⓑ Ⓒ Ⓓ | | 60. | Ⓐ Ⓑ Ⓒ Ⓓ | | | |

Name: _____          Date: _____

STATE PORTION

| 1. | Ⓐ Ⓑ Ⓒ Ⓓ | 31. | Ⓐ Ⓑ Ⓒ Ⓓ |
|---|---|---|---|
| 2. | Ⓐ Ⓑ Ⓒ Ⓓ | 32. | Ⓐ Ⓑ Ⓒ Ⓓ |
| 3. | Ⓐ Ⓑ Ⓒ Ⓓ | 33. | Ⓐ Ⓑ Ⓒ Ⓓ |
| 4. | Ⓐ Ⓑ Ⓒ Ⓓ | 34. | Ⓐ Ⓑ Ⓒ Ⓓ |
| 5. | Ⓐ Ⓑ Ⓒ Ⓓ | 35. | Ⓐ Ⓑ Ⓒ Ⓓ |
| 6. | Ⓐ Ⓑ Ⓒ Ⓓ | | |
| 7. | Ⓐ Ⓑ Ⓒ Ⓓ | | |
| 8. | Ⓐ Ⓑ Ⓒ Ⓓ | | |
| 9. | Ⓐ Ⓑ Ⓒ Ⓓ | | |
| 10. | Ⓐ Ⓑ Ⓒ Ⓓ | | |
| 11. | Ⓐ Ⓑ Ⓒ Ⓓ | | |
| 12. | Ⓐ Ⓑ Ⓒ Ⓓ | | |
| 13. | Ⓐ Ⓑ Ⓒ Ⓓ | | |
| 14. | Ⓐ Ⓑ Ⓒ Ⓓ | | |
| 15. | Ⓐ Ⓑ Ⓒ Ⓓ | | |
| 16. | Ⓐ Ⓑ Ⓒ Ⓓ | | |
| 17 | Ⓐ Ⓑ Ⓒ Ⓓ | | |
| 18. | Ⓐ Ⓑ Ⓒ Ⓓ | | |
| 19. | Ⓐ Ⓑ Ⓒ Ⓓ | | |
| 20. | Ⓐ Ⓑ Ⓒ Ⓓ | | |
| 21. | Ⓐ Ⓑ Ⓒ Ⓓ | | |
| 22. | Ⓐ Ⓑ Ⓒ Ⓓ | | |
| 23. | Ⓐ Ⓑ Ⓒ Ⓓ | | |
| 24. | Ⓐ Ⓑ Ⓒ Ⓓ | | |
| 25. | Ⓐ Ⓑ Ⓒ Ⓓ | | |
| 26. | Ⓐ Ⓑ Ⓒ Ⓓ | | |
| 27. | Ⓐ Ⓑ Ⓒ Ⓓ | | |
| 28. | Ⓐ Ⓑ Ⓒ Ⓓ | | |
| 29. | Ⓐ Ⓑ Ⓒ Ⓓ | | |
| 30. | Ⓐ Ⓑ Ⓒ Ⓓ | | |

## National Portion

1. What is the name given to the estimate amount on a mortgage?

   A. Pre-approval
   B. Post-approval
   C. Principal
   D. Mortgage

2. What is the actual amount of space a tenant can lay carpet and place furniture?

   A. Usable Square Footage
   B. Rentable square footage
   C. Common areas
   D. Service areas

3. What is the name given to an amount of money borrowed to facilitate the purchase of a property?

   A. Escrow
   B. Interest
   C. Down payment
   D. Principal

4. What type of mortgage loan is made available through the United States Department of Veterans Affairs?

   A. Blanket mortgage
   B. Balloon mortgage
   C. Graduated mortgage
   D. VA mortgage

5. What is the value obtained by deducting applied payments from original amortization?

   A. Full term
   B. Paid term
   C. Principal term
   D. Remaining term

6. What is the arrangement that allows a seller to lease a property from a purchaser after selling it?

   A. Leaseback
   B. Leasehold
   C. Sublease
   D. Proprietary lease

7. What type of easement attaches rights to a tenant instead of the land?

   A. Easement appurtenant
   B. Easement in gross
   C. Prescriptive easement
   D. All the above

8. What is the penalty charge for paying back a loan ahead of the scheduled payment plan?

   A. Defaulting penalty
   B. Interest
   C. Prepayment penalty
   D. Principal amount

9. What is an insurance premium paid by the buyer to the lender in order to protect the lender from default on a mortgage?

   A. Hazard insurance
   B. Homeowner's insurance
   C. Private mortgage insurance
   D. Title insurance

10. What is the name given to a party that acts in conjunction with a lender to originate a loan?

   A. Mortgage broker
   B. Third party originator
   C. Lender
   D. Intermediate

11. What is the term used to describe the alteration of a property in order to increase its market value?

   A. Capital Improvement
   B. Preventive maintenance
   C. Appreciation
   D. Common charges

12. What is the tax levied on transfer of property?

   A. Capital gains tax
   B. Deductible tax
   C. Property tax
   D. Transfer tax

13. Which of the following is an appraisal method in real estate?

   A. Sales Comparison Approach
   B. Cost Approach
   C. Income Approach
   D. All of the above

14. For at least how long must an asset be held before being sold to be categorized as long-term capital gains?

   A. One month
   B. Six months
   C. One year
   D. Two years

15. Which of these is considered an operating expense?

   A. Repairs
   B. Depreciation
   C. Payroll
   D. All of the above

16. What is an unlawful detainer?

   A. Forcing rent payments for tenants who have already moved out
   B. Refusing to leave a property despite expiration or termination of lease
   C. Listing a property whose lease has not expired
   D. Subletting a property without permission from the landlord

**17.** What is the freeze placed on a mortgage loan for a period of time?

    A. Cessation
    B. Amortization
    C. Rate lock
    D. Interest freeze

**18.** What type of lease gives the tenant an option to purchase the property?

    A. Leaseback
    B. Lease option
    C. Leasehold
    D. Gross lease

**19.** What is conditioner capacity?

    A. This is the capacity of an air conditioner to heat or cool the room
    B. The space used up by an air conditioner
    C. The strength of an air conditioner
    D. The cooling capacity of an air conditioner and is measured in tons

**20.** What is the name given to an individual that acts in intermediate for brokers and lenders?

    A. Mortgage broker
    B. Mortgage banker
    C. Attorney
    D. Intermediate

**21.** If a property is taxed at 30% with a tax levy of $105,000, what is its assessed value?

    A. $136,500
    B. $146,666
    C. $350,000
    D. None of the above

**22.** What is the notice given when a tenant has a pet in a complex that has no pets policy?

    A. Notice to cure
    B. Notice to quit
    C. Notice of default
    D. Notice of termination

**23.** What is a roof's vertical rise in inches divided by its horizontal span in feet?

    A. Depth
    B. Width
    C. Pitch
    D. Length

**24.** Who engages the services of a broker?

    A. The client
    B. The neighbor
    C. The contractor
    D. The appraiser

**25.** Right of way would be best defined as?

    A.   Escheat
    B.   Easement
    C.   Right of ingress
    D.   Encumbrance

**26.** Who can get partial exemptions from property taxes?

    A.   Disabled
    B.   Schools
    C.   Shelters
    D.   Markets

**27.** What age must a person be to get a Real Estate license?

    A.   16 years
    B.   18 years
    C.   30 years
    D.   43 years

**28.** Which electricity conductor plays the same role as a circuit board?

    A.   Cell
    B.   Capacitor
    C.   Fuse
    D.   Switch

**29.** What is the definition of a bilateral contract?

    A.   A contract that involves only the promisor
    B.   A contract that involves only the promisee
    C.   A contract that involves both a promisor and promisee
    D.   A contract that allows both parties to drop all claims and get out of the contract

**30.** What is real property tax based on?

    A.   Assessed value
    B.   CMA
    C.   Appraisal
    D.   Taxable value

**31.** What agency is responsible for protecting wetlands?

    A.   CERCLA
    B.   Environmental Protection Agency
    C.   FEMA
    D.   NY Health Department

**32.** What is a schedule of the projected future income and expenses for a real estate investment?

    A.   IOU
    B.   Invoice
    C.   Promissory note
    D.   Pro Forma Statement

33. What is an agent required to do if a client refuses to sign an agency disclosure form?

    A. Terminate relationship
    B. Create record of refusal in writing
    C. Continue without record of the refusal
    D. Take legal action against the client

34. What is a general voluntary lien?

    A. Mortgage
    B. Taxes
    C. Revenues
    D. Duties

35. If a salesperson's commission is not paid, he resorts to?

    A. Buyer
    B. Seller
    C. Broker
    D. Lender

36. What type of tenancy exists where property is owned by a single individual?

    A. Joint tenancy
    B. Ownership in severalty
    C. Tenancy in entirety
    D. Tenancy in common

37. Who are testers in real estate?

    A. People who pose as real estate clients to check if fair housing is being practiced
    B. People who assess the value of a property
    C. People who pose as borrowers to ensure proper loaning practices
    D. People who approach the seller without the intention of buying

38. What is the term used to describe the natural increase of land?

    A. Expansion
    B. Avulsion
    C. Erosion
    D. Accretion

39. What is the length of time allowed for depreciation for a residential property?

    A. 5 years
    B. 27.5 years
    C. 39 years
    D. 70 years

40. What is the term used to describe personal property?

    A. Chattel
    B. Investment
    C. Possession
    D. Real property

**41.** Which act was enacted to ensure parties involved in a real estate transaction receive complete settlement cost disclosure?

    A.   RESPA
    B.   FHA
    C.   Clean Water Act
    D.   Civil Rights Act

**42.** What is the name given to the downward movement of water through soil?

    A.   Absorption
    B.   Filtration
    C.   Percolation
    D.   Proration

**43.** What type of income is generated by investing in a limited partnership?

    A.   Active income
    B.   Passive income
    C.   Surplus income
    D.   Savings

**44.** What mortgage type allows the mortgagor to make payments only on the interest accrued?

    A.   Blanket mortgage
    B.   Balloon mortgage
    C.   Graduated mortgage
    D.   Straight term mortgage

**45.** Mary's agent helped her purchase a property and negotiated a mortgage for her. This agent also represented the seller. What type of agent did Mary engage?

    A.   Single agent
    B.   Dual agent
    C.   Double agent
    D.   None of the above

**46.** What is the land survey process that involves the surveyor starting at an easily identifiable point and describing the property in terms of courses and distances and eventually returning to the starting point?

    A.   ALTA
    B.   Boundary construction
    C.   Metes and bounds
    D.   Topographic surveys

**47.** What arrangement allows the seller to absorb an existing loan in order to allow the buyer another mortgage?

    A.   Simple mortgage
    B.   Wraparound mortgage
    C.   Mortgage by conditional sale
    D.   Reverse mortgage

**48.** Which real estate participants are legally required to be licensed?

    A.   Sellers
    B.   Buyers
    C.   Lenders
    D.   Real estate agents and brokers

**49.** What is the term used to refer to the act of mixing money belonging to a client with one's own funds?

A. Commingling
B. Investing
C. Stealing
D. Saving

**50.** What is the effect of a larger money supply on the interest rates?

A. They decrease
B. They increase
C. Remains constant
D. They have no relationship

**51.** What is a homeowner's policy that covers two parts: property and liability?

A. HO1
B. HO2
C. HO3
D. HO4

**52.** What is the name given to tax calculated based on the value of an asset?

A. Ad valorem tax
B. Property tax
C. Capital gains tax
D. Transfer tax

**53.** What kind of lease agreement requires the landlord to pay for all expenses?

A. Gross lease
B. Ground lease
C. Net lease
D. Sublease

**54.** If a seller nets $442,000 from the sale of her home, and the commission is 5%, how much did the home sell for?

A. $464,100
B. $420,952
C. $459,680
D. None of the above

**55.** What is the short-term loan that covers the interval between selling one property and buying another?

A. Bridge Loan
B. Cash flow
C. Cash on cash return
D. Mortgage

**56.** What are the set rules established for condominium or co-op tenants?

A. House rules
B. Investment agreement
C. Regulations
D. Policy

**57.** Who is responsible for the rent in a sublease?

    A.  New tenant
    B.  Lessee
    C.  Lessor
    D.  Roommate

**58.** What income type does a salary fall under?

    A.  Active income
    B.  Passive income
    C.  Savings
    D.  Investment

**59.** What is the name given to an estate that gives the holder temporary possession rights?

    A.  Concurrent estates
    B.  Estate for years
    C.  Freehold estates
    D.  Leasehold estate

**60.** What is a permit issued to a builder stating the property is fit for occupancy?

    A.  Certificate of occupancy
    B.  Contract of sale
    C.  Landmark designation
    D.  Receipt of sales deposit

**61.** What kind of mortgage pays off the principal?

    A.  Amortized loan
    B.  Fixed- rate loan
    C.  Floating rate loan
    D.  Mortgage

**62.** What is the income that is left after all operating costs are paid in a real estate investment?

    A.  Investment
    B.  Net operating income
    C.  Profit
    D.  Revenue

**63.** Which lease allows for changes in rent within the lease term?

    A.  Graduated lease
    B.  Lease break
    C.  Sublease
    D.  Value point

**64.** What is the married couple's capital gains tax exclusion on the sale of their primary home?

    A.  $50,000
    B.  $75,000
    C.  $250,000
    D.  $500,000

**65.** What should a licensee do with their pocket card?

    A. Advertise it

    B. Carry a physical copy or have a digital image on a device

    C. File it

    D. Use it to get clients

**66.** You must have a real estate license for all of the following activities **EXCEPT**:

    A. Selling a mobile home not affixed to the land

    B. Selling a commercial property

    C. Selling a residential property

    D. Representing a client who wants to rent

**67.** What is a single person's capital gains tax exclusion?

    A. $25,000

    B. $100,000

    C. $250,000

    D. $500,000

**68.** What is the term given to violation of neighbor's property by trespassing?

    A. Easement

    B. Escheat

    C. Encroachment

    D. Encumbrance

**69.** What type of insurance is referred to as renter's insurance?

    A. HO1

    B. HO2

    C. HO3

    D. HO4

**70.** What is a form of co-ownership by which all parties have undivided interests in the property but no right of survivorship?

    A. Tenancy in common

    B. Tenancy in entirety

    C. Joint tenancy

    D. Ownership in severalty

**71.** What conveys a grantor's interest in real property?

    A. Deed

    B. Insurance

    C. Title

    D. Warrant

**72.** What is the chain of deeds and other documents used in transferring title of land from one owner to another consecutively?

    A. Abstract of title

    B. Deed chain

    C. History of deed

    D. Chain of title

**73.** If you paid a down payment of $200,000 for a property worth $1,000,000 dollars and you currently rent it out for $4,000 a month, what is the cash on cash return?

    A.   4%
    B.   4.8%
    C.   20%
    D.   24%

**74.** What is a Certificate of Eligibility?

    A.   Certificate that shows one is to be exempt from property tax
    B.   Certificate that is presented by veterans to show proof that they have met the minimum service requirements to be eligible for a VA loan
    C.   Certificate that shows a construction is fit for occupancy
    D.   Certificate that shows merit

**75.** What is the insurance policy that protects a lender from loss due to disputes over ownership of a property and defects in the title?

    A.   Hazard insurance
    B.   Home warranty
    C.   Homeowner's insurance
    D.   Title insurance

**76.** Property that has a divided form of ownership is called?

    A.   Cooperative
    B.   Planned unit development
    C.   Time-share
    D.   Joint tenants

**77.** What is the definition of a syndication?

    A.   Income that is earned by a spouse prior to marriage
    B.   Land that is divided into smaller pieces of land
    C.   Mutual funds that invest in rental properties
    D.   Real estate that is purchased by a group which includes at least one sponsor and several investors

**78.** Which of the following is **not** an essential element of a contract?

    A.   Notarized signature
    B.   Consideration
    C.   Agreement by offer and acceptance
    D.   Competent parties

**79.** Which listing agreement allows the owner of the listed property to sell the property on their own and not have to pay commission to the listing broker?

    A.   Open listing
    B.   Option listing
    C.   Exclusive agency listing
    D.   Both A and C

**80.** What is the listing agreement that gives the broker the payment of commission no matter who sells the property?

    A.   Entirety
    B.   Exclusive-right-to-sell listing
    C.   Open listing
    D.   Net Listing

**THIS IS THE END OF THE NATIONAL PORTION.**

## State Portion

1. The Michigan Home Solicitation Sales Act gives a consumer 3 business days to cancel a contract if _____.

   A. A gift was offered for attending a sales presentation which then led to the contract
   B. A consumer's primary home is used as security and the loan is not used to construct or purchase the home
   C. The sale was solicited in the consumer's home
   D. All of the above

2. According to the Michigan Condominium Act, a new condo construction agreement is binding 9 days after the developer delivers which of the following documents to the purchaser?

   A. 5-year projection of HOA fees
   B. The Condominium Buyer's Handbook
   C. The blueprints of the property
   D. All of the above

3. Which of the following statements is true about penalties sanctioned by the Michigan Board of Real Estate Brokers and Salespersons?

   A. A first offense penalty fine cannot be more than 500 dollars
   B. Penalties are assessed by courts
   C. A second offense penalty cannot exceed 1 year of jail time
   D. All of the above

4. This state law defines price fixing as unreasonable.

   A. Federal Uniform State Act
   B. Michigan Uniform State Antitrust Act
   C. Michigan Uniform Act
   D. There is no such state law

5. The state requires most people to have a license to conduct real estate services. Which of the following persons requires a license to sell or lease property?

   A. Individual owners
   B. Individual lessors
   C. The son of an elderly owner
   D. Developers who are selling property they built

6. The _____ governs interest rates for various types of loans and lenders?

   A. Michigan Board of Real Estate Brokers and Salespersons
   B. Michigan Uniform State Antitrust Act
   C. Michigan General Usury Statute
   D. None of the above

7. Which law replaced the Michigan 1968 Fair Housing Act and provided 9 categories of protection, include marital status?

   A. Persons with Disabilities Act
   B. Elliot-Larsen Civil Rights Act
   C. Truth in Lending Act
   D. Home Improvement Finance Act

8. Michigan requires its appraisers to obtain a licensure. Which of the following is not necessary to take the state licensed real estate appraiser exam?

   A. Good moral character
   B. 150 hours of approved prelicensure appraiser education
   C. 200 hours of experience over a 6-month period
   D. 18 years of age

**9.** To maintain a license a Michigan Appraiser must renew their license every 2 years. How many hours of continuing education is needed to renew?

    A.   14 class hours for each year during the period preceding the renewal

    B.   30 class hours during each renewal period

    C.   20 class hours during each renewal period

    D.   25 class hours for each year during the period preceding the renewal

**10.** A _____ is where the land survey description begins.

    A.   Point of beginning

    B.   Starting point

    C.   Beginning point

    D.   Start of property

**11.** 1 section of land is equal to _____.

    A.   640 feet

    B.   640 acres

    C.   640 miles

    D.   640 kilometers

**12.** Which law requires a local government review for land that has been divided into parcels less than 40 acres?

    A.   Exempt split act

    B.   Division act

    C.   Plat act

    D.   Land division act

**13.** Which of the following is not a type of freehold estate?

    A. Fee simple
    B. Defeasible fee
    C. Life estate
    D. All of the above

**14.** Which of the following is a type of ownership?

    A. Severalty
    B. Joint
    C. Entirety
    D. All of the above

**15.** The rights to enjoy an ocean that is on to property is called _____.

    A. Riparian rights
    B. Littoral rights
    C. Accretion
    D. Reliction

**16.** The _____ is a law that may terminate mineral interest that have been separated from the surface ownership if certain conditions have been met.

    A. Michigan Dormant Mineral Rights Act
    B. Mineral Rights Act
    C. Ownership Act
    D. Dormant Rights Act

**17.** The Wetland Protection Act states that
_____ cannot be done without a permit.

A. Deposit soil
B. Dredge, remove or permit
   removal of materials
C. Construct, operate or maintain
   any use or development
D. All of the above

**18.** A _____ is property that is owned only
during the lifeline of the tenant.

A. Life estate
B. Defeasible fee
C. Life estate
D. None of the above

**19.** These east-west lines offer a reference and
interest the principal meridian.

A. Range lines
B. Base lines
C. Principal meridian
D. Township lines

**20.** Which of the following is a disadvantage of
mete and bounds?

A. They cost a lot of money
B. They can lengthy and complex
C. They are subject to shifting
   monuments
D. B&C only

21. Which of the following statements is true about the seller's disclosure act?

   A. Applies to the sale of one to four family residential property
   B. The form must be filled out by the listing agent
   C. Applies to the sale of all real estate
   D. B&C only

22. Which of the following is a way to transfer real property?

   A. Death
   B. Involuntary alienation
   C. Voluntary alienation
   D. All of the above

23. A fence is an example of a(n) _____.

   A. Commingling
   B. Blockbusting
   C. Appurtenance
   D. Arbitration

24. A checkout lane is an example of a(n) _____.

   A. Appurtenance
   B. Trade fixture
   C. Commingling
   D. Arbitration

**25.** Which of the following is not a type of deed?

    A. Warranty deed
    B. Special warranty deed
    C. Quitclaim deed
    D. All of the above are types of deeds

**26.** The amount a willing purchaser would pay a willing seller is the _____.

    A. Seller's price
    B. Fair market value
    C. Buyer's maximum
    D. Appurtenant

**27.** Which of the following is not a type of licensed appraiser in the state of Michigan?

    A. Limited real estate appraiser
    B. State licensed real estate appraiser
    C. Certified commercial appraiser
    D. Certified general appraiser

**28.** A _____ is used to value rental properties.

    A. Reproduction
    B. Capitalization approach
    C. Gross rent multiplier
    D. Cost approach

29. Which of the following is a principal of appraising?

 A. Substitution
 B. Plottage
 C. Useful life
 D. All of the above

30. A _____ is used to determine the sale price when the seller has a set price they must obtain.

 A. Seller's net math
 B. Deed restriction
 C. Net price
 D. Seller's price

31. Which of the following is a way to terminate an easement?

 A. A merger
 B. An agreement
 C. Abandonment accompanied by end of purpose
 D. All of the above

32. A utility company running a power line through private property is an example of a(n) _____.

 A. Appurtenant easement
 B. Commingling
 C. Easement in gross
 D. Public property

**33.** There are two types of _____, general and specific.

   A.   Judgement
   B.   Liens
   C.   Debt
   D.   None of the above

**34.** A _____ is usually paid for by the seller and names the buyer as beneficiary.

   A.   Owner's title policy
   B.   Buyer's deed
   C.   Buyer's policy
   D.   Owner's deed

**35.** A covenant of seisin is a type of _____.

   A.   Quitclaim deed
   B.   General warranty deed
   C.   Special deed
   D.   None of the above

**THIS IS THE END OF THE STATE PORTION.**

# Answer Key – National Portion

| | | | | | | | |
|---|---|---|---|---|---|---|---|
| 1. | A | 21. | C | 41. | A | 61. | A |
| 2. | A | 22. | A | 42. | C | 62. | B |
| 3. | D | 23. | C | 43. | B | 63. | A |
| 4. | D | 24. | A | 44. | D | 64. | D |
| 5. | D | 25. | B | 45. | B | 65. | B |
| 6. | A | 26. | A | 46. | C | 66. | A |
| 7. | B | 27. | B | 47. | B | 67. | C |
| 8. | C | 28. | C | 48. | D | 68. | C |
| 9. | C | 29. | C | 49. | A | 69. | D |
| 10. | B | 30. | A | 50. | A | 70. | A |
| 11. | A | 31. | B | 51. | C | 71. | A |
| 12. | D | 32. | D | 52. | A | 72. | D |
| 13. | D | 33. | B | 53. | A | 73. | D |
| 14. | C | 34. | A | 54. | D | 74. | B |
| 15. | D | 35. | C | 55. | A | 75. | D |
| 16. | B | 36. | B | 56. | A | 76. | C |
| 17. | C | 37. | A | 57. | B | 77. | D |
| 18. | B | 38. | D | 58. | A | 78. | A |
| 19. | D | 39. | B | 59. | D | 79. | D |
| 20. | A | 40. | A | 60. | A | 80. | B |

1. **A) Pre-approval**

Prior to purchasing a property, the borrower can visit a lender and obtain a pre-approval letter stating the amount of credit the lender is willing to accord the buyer which will help determine what the buyer can afford.

2. **A) Usable Square Footage**

Usable square footage is the amount of space you actually occupy in a leased space.

3. **D) Principal**

The principal is the amount of money that a lender gives a borrower to facilitate property purchase. Payment of principal results in increase in borrower's equity.

4.  **D) VA mortgage**

This is a mortgage plan that is tailored to assist service members and their surviving spouses to become homeowners. There are usually a lot of qualifying standards put in place to be eligible for this type of mortgage and it is usually offered by banks and other credit facilities. The Veteran administration usually acts as a guarantor for the loan. Qualified Veterans are usually eligible for 100% financing.

5.  **D) Remaining term**

It is usually used to complete the period of time left on a loan and the amount of principal payment to be covered within that period.

6.  **A) Leaseback**

This is an arrangement that allows a seller to lease a property from the purchaser on transfer of ownership. The details surrounding the lease arrangement are usually discussed immediately after the sale.

7.  **B) Easement in gross**

Easement in gross is the agreement that attaches rights to the tenant over the property. Transfer of the land results in an immediate termination of the agreement. The agreement can be renegotiated with the new tenant over time.

8.  **C) Prepayment penalty**

This is the penalty placed on the significant payment of a mortgage within the first five years of the loan. This penalty exists to protect lenders from loss of interest income.

9.  **C) Private mortgage insurance**

These insurance payments are usually discontinued once a buyer builds up to 20% equity on the home.

10.  **B) Third party originator**

This is any third party used to originate a loan. Lenders often employ the services of third-party moderators to underwrite and originate loans. They offer no ongoing and lasting responsibility for the mortgage.

 Practice Test

11. **A) Capital Improvement**

This is the addition of a permanent change in a structure or restoration of damaged property. It is done to increase the longevity and market value of the property. For an item to be considered a capital investment, it has to be a permanent addition and capable of improving the value of the property.

12. **D) Transfer tax**

This is any tax that is levied on transfer of ownership or title of property from one individual to another. It is usually non-deductible. It is usually levied at the local or federal level depending on the type of property changing ownership.

13. **D) All of the above**

Sales Comparison Approach, Cost Approach, and Income Approach are all appraisal methods.

14. **C) One year**

An asset must be held for at least one year before selling in order for profits to be categorized as long-term capital gains.

15. **D) All of the above**

Operating expenses include any costs associated with the operation and maintenance of an income-producing property.

16. **B) Refusing to leave a property despite expiration or termination of lease**

Commonly compared to an eviction, which is the legal removal of an individual from a lease due to violation of the terms of the agreement.

17. **C) Rate lock**

This occurs when lenders lock in a rate because it is the lowest rate being offered at the time. It is not a legally binding agreement and borrowers are allowed to abandon the rates based on the rising and falling.

18. **B) Lease option**

A lease option is a lease agreement that gives the tenant a choice to purchase the property within or at the end of the lease. It gives the buyer flexibility to make a purchase on the property. Usually involves an upfront agreement between the tenant and the landlord.

19. **D) The cooling capacity of an air conditioner and is measured in tons**

It is determined by measuring the size of the space being serviced by the air conditioner. The size area of the room is measured and multiplied by 25 BTU to determine the cooling capacity required in an air conditioner.

20. **A) Mortgage broker**

This is an individual that serves as an intermediate between lenders and brokers. A mortgage broker facilitates negotiations of interest rates and takes circulation of paperwork between the lender and the borrowers.

21. **C) $350,000**

$105,000 / 0.3 = $350,000

22. **A) Notice to cure**

This is a notice given to a leaseholder by the landlord regarding participation in activities that are not allowed in the building. The tenant is given 10 days to correct the mistake. Refusal to make adjustment results in the tenant being served a notice of termination.

23. **C) Pitch**

Defines the steepness of a roof. It is used to determine the material used for roofing and the space in the attic. It is also used to determine stability so that corrective measures can be undertaken early.

24. **A) The client**

A broker is required to work in the best interests of the client to ensure the best possible deal for the client.

25. **B) Easement**

This is the right to use another person's land temporarily without actually possessing it.

26. **A) Disabled**

Disabled, veterans, elderly, farmers, Gold Star Parents, and Star Program Homeowners. The above classes of people can get partial tax exemption by having the values of their homes reduced translating in reduced property taxes.

27. **B) 18 years**

This is the minimum required age for a real estate agent that has taken the education course and passed the qualifying exam.

28. **C) Fuse**

A fuse is a small conductor that is designed to melt under high current to break the circuit. A fuse should always maintain a series connection to the component of the circuit.

29. **C) A contract that involves both a promisor and promisee**

This contract occurs when both parties exchange a promise for a promise. Both parties enter into an agreement to fulfill their side of the bargain. Each party is also an obligor and obligee in this type of contract.

30. **A) Assessed value**

Assessed value is the monetary value assigned to a property and is usually used to determine the value of a property for the purpose of taxation.

31. **B) Environmental Protection Agency**

The Environmental Protection Agency is tasked with protecting both human and environmental health. The agency creates standards and laws promoting health of individuals and the environment and participates in upholding them by administering correcting efforts like CERCLA.

32. **D) Pro Forma Statement**

This is an estimate summary of income production if the current trends are maintained. This is usually in multifamily properties in order to help the investor understand general financial operations of the property.

33. **B) Create record of refusal in writing**

In the case where a client refuses to sign a disclosure, the agent is required to clearly state the names of the client and the facts surrounding the refusal to sign the disclosure. An agent is also required to sign a declaration in the presence of a notary public and have it notarized.

34. **A) Mortgage**

A voluntary lien is a claim a debtor has over the property of another and is initiated by the debtor as in the case of a mortgage. The debtor cannot legally sell the property as it is considered collateral.

35. **C) Broker**

An agent resorts to a broker for commission as the law does not allow salespersons to work independently and therefore cannot be paid directly. A broker on receiving commission from the sale of the property is required to split the commission amongst the agents that were involved in the transaction.

36. **B) Ownership in severalty**

This is a situation where real estate is owned by a single person or entity providing the owner with the most control of the land. A sole owner is at will to take any action on the land such as selling or leasing.

37. **A) People who pose as real estate clients to check if fair housing is being practiced**

Testing was initiated under the Fair Housing Act to ensure that housing providers act in accordance with the fair housing laws that protect against discrimination based on race, origin and gender.

38. **D) Accretion**

This is the natural growth of a parcel of land due to mother nature. It occurs due to accumulation of soil on the shoreline of a water body. A decrease due to erosion is also possible.

39. **B) 27.5 years**

Depreciation is the loss of value of a property due to age, wear and tear. A residential property can only declare depreciation after 27.5 years in order to reduce the value of the property and property tax on the property.

40. **A) Chattel**

A chattel is a tangible property which is either mobile or immobile. However, this term cannot be used to describe real estate holdings.

41. **A) RESPA**

The Real Estate Settling Procedures Act was developed in order to protect the parties involved in a real estate transaction from abuse during the settlement process. The act mandates lenders and brokers to disclose all matters crucial to the transaction service, settlement service and consumer protection laws

42. **C) Percolation**

This is the process in which water reaches the subsoil and roots. The pore space present in soil acts as a medium for the water to percolate. The ability of water to move through soil is dependent on the soil texture and structure. Some soils allow water to move very deep into the ground which may result in mixing with underground water reservoirs.

43. **B) Passive income**

This is income that is generated with minimal activity. It requires little to no effort to earn on a daily basis.

44. **D) Straight term mortgage**

A straight term mortgage is a mortgage that allows the mortgagor to make monthly payments on the interest accrued throughout the mortgage's lifespan. The principal remains unpaid until a set date where it becomes due for payment in full.

45. **B) Dual agent**

Mary's agent was able to perform the above transactions for her because he was working for both the Mary and the seller of the property.

46. **C) Metes and bounds**

This is a legal principle of land description and uses natural and artificial landmarks as boundaries. It is often used to describe irregular tracts of land. Metes defines straight line distances while bounds defines a less regular but identifiable lines. Measurements from an original point that is a monument and metes and bounds are described taking into account the boundaries. The process is repeated until the surveyor returns to the original point.

47. **B) Wraparound mortgage**

Wraparound mortgages are used to refinance property. They are mini loans that include the balance of the preexisting mortgage and an additional loan to cover the new property. The seller is granted a promissory note highlighting the amount due.

48. **D) Real estate agents and brokers**

They need to be licensed as they legally represent clients, buyers and sellers, in transferring ownership of property.

49. **A) Commingling**

This is a breach of trust that occurs when a representative of a client mixes individual funds with that of the client making it impossible to determine the amounts that belong to each individual.

50. **A) They decrease**

Money supply is influenced by supply and demand. An increase in the money supply will result in a decreased interest rate making it easier to borrow and vice versa. Therefore, money and interest rates have an inversely proportional relationship.

51. **C) HO3**

A home owner's policy is a property insurance that covers losses and damages done to the insured's house and assets within the home. It also provides liability coverage against accidents within the home.

52. **A) Ad valorem tax**

This is the tax levied by a municipality or local government entity based on assessed value. A public assessor is engaged to value the property in order to calculate the tax owed.

53. **A) Gross lease**

This is a flat rent fee that included all expenses associated with ownership. It is inclusive of incidental charges such as taxes, insurance and utilities. It is an uncommon lease as landlords are unaware of the utility charges that may be incurred by a tenant.

54. **D) None of the above**

$442,000 / (1 - 0.05) = $465,263

55. **A) Bridge Loan**

This is a short-term loan of up to one year that provides cash flow enabling an individual to meet current obligations while awaiting permanent financing. It is often used in real estate to purchase a new home while awaiting the sale of the old property.

56. **A) House rules**

These are set rules that have been put in place to ensure the comfort of the tenants living within the building. Violation of the house rules clause may result in eviction.

57. **B) Lessee**

The original tenant for rent as he/she is liable to the owner. In case of overdue rent by the new tenant, the original tenant is held accountable.

58. **A) Active income**

This is an income earned from performing services. Active participation is required to yield payment.

59. **D) Leasehold estate**

This is a lease that allows the tenant to have real property for an extended period of time. A time frame is agreed upon in the lease and the tenant is allowed to erect structures and profit from the business that has been established at the site.

60. **A) Certificate of occupancy**

This is a legal statement issued by the building department clearing a building for occupancy on meeting the building codes and other laws that surround the construction of a residential or commercial building. It can be obtained when a new building is constructed or an old building is repurposed.

61. **A) Amortized loan**

An amortized loan is a loan with a scheduled payment over a period of time that pays off the interest and principal. An amortized loan payment schedule focuses on paying off the interest and progresses into the principal.

62. **B) Net operating income**

This is a method used to value the income generating properties. To obtain the value, all expenses incurred during operations is subtracted to the total income produced by the property. To get the true value produced by the property, revenues earned must be included.

63. **A) Graduated lease**

A graduated lease is an agreement between the landlord and tenant that allows for periodic adjustment of monthly payments based on the market value of the property. It stands to benefit the landlord over a long period of time.

64. **D) $500,000**

In accordance with the Taxpayers Relief Act, a married couple is eligible for exclusion from capital gain tax for profits of up to $500,000. This is provided the property sold is a primary residence, they have been living in it for at least 2 years.

65. **B) Carry a physical copy or have a digital image on a device**

A pocket card is a pocket-sized license identifying the holder as a licensed agent. It contains a photo, name and business address of the holder.

66. **A) Selling a mobile home not affixed to the land**

If the mobile home is sitting on a leased lot, then it is considered as personal property and can therefore be sold like a car or other personal belongings.

67. **C) $250,000**

According to the Taxpayers relief act, a single person is eligible for a capital gains tax exemption for profits of up to $250,000 on the sale of a primary home.

68. **C) Encroachment**

Encroachment is a violation of property rights that occurs when an individual chooses to ignore set boundaries. This can be by extending structure into the neighbor's land or illegally entering the neighbor's property.

69. **D) HO4**

This insurance is designed to protect the insured and belongings from the covered losses. It covers liability, personal property, additional living expenses and medical payments to others. The insurance covers against risks specified in the policy.

70. **A) Tenancy in common**

A tenancy in common is a legal agreement where two or more people with undivided rights own a property. Members of a tenancy in common are not mandated to have equal rights and can enter the agreement at any time. Members of a tenancy in common are free to leave their shares to a beneficiary.

71. **A) Deed**

This is a signed legal document that conveys interest of a property and is used in cases of transfer of property provided a set of conditions are met. For a deed to hold legal merit, it must be filed in a public record.

72. **D) Chain of title**

This is an official ownership record of a property. It is usually maintained from a centralized registry. It is used widely to protect lenders and buyers from losses occurring due to errors in the title report.

73. **D) 24%**

($4,000 * 12) / $200,000 = 0.24

74. **B) Certificate that is presented by veterans to show proof that they have met the minimum service requirements to be eligible for a VA loan**

The Certificate of Eligibility serves as proof of a veteran's military service and must be provided to lenders during the VA loan process

75.     **D) Title insurance**

A title insurance is based on the indemnity clause. It is taken by a buyer to protect the lender from loss caused by unidentified defects in the title. It acts against traditional insurance by protecting clients against claims on a past occurrence

76.     **C) Time-share**

Also called vacation ownership, a time-share is shared ownership of a property. This type of property is typically a vacation property i.e. a condominium in a resort area. The buyer typically purchases a certain period of time for the unit, typically one- to two-week periods.

77.     **D) Real estate that is purchased by a group which includes at least one sponsor and several investors**

Syndication is a method investors can use to invest in properties. Investors pool their financial and intellectual resources together to invest in properties that they would not be able to invest in individually.

78.     **A) Notarized signature**

A notarized signature is not necessary in a contract. A legal purpose, competent parties, offer and acceptance, consideration and consent are the essential elements of a contract.

79.     **D) Both A and C**

Exclusive agency listing is an agreement between a real estate firm and seller which grants the firm the exclusive rights to sell the property but also allows the seller to sell the home without paying a commission to the listing agent. An open listing is a property listing using multiple real estate agents. This type of listing also allows an owner to list and sell the property without paying a commission to an agent.

80.     **B) Exclusive-right-to-sell listing**

A legal agreement under which the seller agrees to pay a commission to the listing broker. The listing broker acts as the agent and is provided commission whether the property is sold through the listing broker, seller or anyone else. An exception occurs when the seller names one or more individuals/entities as exemptions in the listing agreement.

## Answer Key – State Portion

| | | | |
|---|---|---|---|
| 1. | D | 21. | A |
| 2. | B | 22. | D |
| 3. | D | 23. | C |
| 4. | B | 24. | B |
| 5. | C | 25. | D |
| 6. | C | 26. | B |
| 7. | B | 27. | C |
| 8. | C | 28. | C |
| 9. | A | 29. | D |
| 10. | A | 30. | A |
| 11. | B | 31. | D |
| 12. | D | 32. | C |
| 13. | D | 33. | B |
| 14. | D | 34. | A |
| 15. | B | 35. | B |
| 16. | A | | |
| 17. | D | | |
| 18. | A | | |
| 19. | B | | |
| 20. | D | | |

1.  **D) All of the above**

    All of the above is true. A consumer has 1 day to cancel a contract if the contract is for a home improvement and the consumer agrees to make payments over time to the contractor.

2.  **B) The Condominium Buyer's Handbook**

    This along with the recorded master deed with attached bylaws and sub plans, a copy of the purchase and escrow agreements, and a disclosure statement are required to close a new condo sale.

3.  **D) All of the above**

    All of the above is true about penalties sanctioned by the Board. The board also only has 60 days to meet and determine the penalties. A first offense jail time cannot exceed 90 days and the second offense fine cannot exceed 1,000 dollars.

4.    **B) Michigan Uniform State Antitrust Act**

This law states certain types or trade restraints are so injurious to competition that there can be no justification. Price fixing, boycotts and concerted refusal to deal are among the banned.

5.    **C) Son of an elderly owner**

The son of an elderly owner cannot sell a home on behalf of his parents and an individual owner cannot sell the property if there have been more than 6 owners in a 12-month period.

6.    **C) Michigan General Usury Statute**

This state law states that charging more than the maximum interest rate is considered usury or criminal.

7.    **B) Elliot-Larsen Civil Rights Act**

This law prohibits discrimination and provides 9 categories of   race, color, religion, national origin, sex, disability, familial status, age, and marital status.

8.    **C) 200 hours of experience over a 6-month period**

200 hours of experience over a 6-month period is not true, a prospective appraiser must complete 1,000 hours of experience. Out of the 150 hours of education, 15 hours must be in a National USPAP course.

9.    **A) 14 class hours for each year during the period preceding the renewal**

14 hours for each year or 28 hours during each renewal period is required to keep an appraiser's license.

10.    **A) Point of beginning**

The point of beginning is where the survey description begins and is typically established at a clearly defined monument. i.e. one corner of the property's boundaries.

11.    **B) 640 acres**

1 section is equal to 640 acres and 1 township to 36 sections.

12.    **D) Land division act**

This law states that any division of land that results in one or more of the parcels being less than 40 acres is subject to local government review.

13.   **D) All of the above**

A freehold estate is one of the two ways land is divided. Freehold estates can then be divided into fee simple, defeasible fee and life estate.

14.   **D) All of the above**

All of the listed are types of ownership based on the number of owners. The other type of ownership is common.

15.   **B) Littoral rights**

Littoral rights attach to the land and once the land is sold the right to enjoy the water goes to the new landowner.

16.   **A) Michigan Dormant Mineral Rights Act**

These rights are terminated if rights have not been shown on record in the past 20 years and have not had any permits or production occur within the past 20 years on that parcel.

17.   **D) All of the above**

The permit must be provided by the Department of Environmental Quality. Other activities that are not permitted is the draining of surface water from a wetland and permitting the placing of fill removal from a wetland.

18.   **A) Life estate**

A life estate is ownership of property but only during the lifetime of the tenant. The owner of the life estate is called a life tenant.

19.   **B) Base lines**

This is the principal east and west line that all rectangular survey in define areas are based.

20.   **D) B&C only**

Mete and bounds use natural or artificial monuments such as trees, boulders, and stakes as markers.

21.   **A) Applies to the sale of one to four family residential property**

This act does not apply to all real estate sales. The seller is required to fill out the form and failure to provide the disclosure to the buyer can result in the buyer voiding the contract.

22.     **D) All of the above**

All of the above are ways to transfer real property.

23.     **C) Appurtenance**

An appurtenance is anything that is tangible or intangible, real, or personal and is said to run with the land.

24.     **B) Trade fixture**

This is an item that is used in one's business and no matter how attached, it remains personal property. Other examples are store counters and shelving units.

25.     **D) All of the above are types of deeds**

A warranty deed, special warranty deed and a quitclaim deed are all types of deeds.

26.     **B) Fair market value**

This is what the purchaser is willing to pay a seller. It is exclusive of reasonable fees and costs of purchase.

27.     **C) Certified commercial appraiser**

An appraiser must learn how to do a market analysis. Another type of appraiser is a certified residential appraiser.

28.     **C) Gross rent multiplier**

This is used to value rental properties by using a monthly multiplier.

29.     **D) All of the above**

A conformity and contribution are also types of principals of appraising.

30.     **A) Seller's net math**

The element of the seller's net math is part or the seller's net or share, total or sale price, and rate or seller's percent.

31.     **D) All of the above**

A merger, abandonment that has been accompanied by end of purpose and agreement are all ways to end an easement.

32. **C) Easement in gross**

An easement in gross has no benefit to the parcel land. The utility company, in the example, is the benefited party.

33. **B) Liens**

A lien is a hold on a person's property for a debt or other obligation. An example is a general lien placed on a person's property because income taxes were not paid.

34. **A) Owner's title policy**

This also indemnifies the buyer against loss and should be in the around of the purchase price.

35. **B) General warranty deed**

A covenant of warranty forever, further assurance, against encumbrances, quiet enjoyment and seisin are all types of warranty deeds.

# Practice Test 4

Directions:

1. You have a 3-hour time limit to complete the whole exam.

2. To pass, you must answer at least 70% of all questions correctly.

3. Some questions will require mathematics. You may use a calculator.

4. **Phones and pagers are not allowed. Having either will result in automatic dismissal from the exam and nullification of exam scores.**

Tips:

- Answer all questions even if you are unsure.
- Mark any questions you are stuck on and revisit them after you are done. The exam is timed so make sure you finish as many questions as you can.
- After reading the question, try answering it in your head first to avoid getting confused by the choices.
- Read the entire question before looking at the answers.
- Use the process of elimination to filter out choices that don't seem correct to increase your chances of selecting the correct answer.
- Be aware of important keywords like **not, sometimes, always**, and **never**. These words completely alter the ask of the question so it's important to keep track of them.

**PLEASE READ THESE INSTRUCTIONS CAREFULLY.**

# Practice Test 4

Name: _____          Date: _____

## NATIONAL PORTION

| | | | | | | | | | | | | |
|---|---|---|---|---|---|---|---|---|---|---|---|---|
| 1. | Ⓐ Ⓑ Ⓒ Ⓓ | 31. | Ⓐ Ⓑ Ⓒ Ⓓ | 61. | Ⓐ Ⓑ Ⓒ Ⓓ |
| 2. | Ⓐ Ⓑ Ⓒ Ⓓ | 32. | Ⓐ Ⓑ Ⓒ Ⓓ | 62. | Ⓐ Ⓑ Ⓒ Ⓓ |
| 3. | Ⓐ Ⓑ Ⓒ Ⓓ | 33. | Ⓐ Ⓑ Ⓒ Ⓓ | 63. | Ⓐ Ⓑ Ⓒ Ⓓ |
| 4. | Ⓐ Ⓑ Ⓒ Ⓓ | 34. | Ⓐ Ⓑ Ⓒ Ⓓ | 64. | Ⓐ Ⓑ Ⓒ Ⓓ |
| 5. | Ⓐ Ⓑ Ⓒ Ⓓ | 35. | Ⓐ Ⓑ Ⓒ Ⓓ | 65. | Ⓐ Ⓑ Ⓒ Ⓓ |
| 6. | Ⓐ Ⓑ Ⓒ Ⓓ | 36. | Ⓐ Ⓑ Ⓒ Ⓓ | 66. | Ⓐ Ⓑ Ⓒ Ⓓ |
| 7. | Ⓐ Ⓑ Ⓒ Ⓓ | 37. | Ⓐ Ⓑ Ⓒ Ⓓ | 67. | Ⓐ Ⓑ Ⓒ Ⓓ |
| 8. | Ⓐ Ⓑ Ⓒ Ⓓ | 38. | Ⓐ Ⓑ Ⓒ Ⓓ | 68. | Ⓐ Ⓑ Ⓒ Ⓓ |
| 9. | Ⓐ Ⓑ Ⓒ Ⓓ | 39. | Ⓐ Ⓑ Ⓒ Ⓓ | 69. | Ⓐ Ⓑ Ⓒ Ⓓ |
| 10. | Ⓐ Ⓑ Ⓒ Ⓓ | 40. | Ⓐ Ⓑ Ⓒ Ⓓ | 70. | Ⓐ Ⓑ Ⓒ Ⓓ |
| 11. | Ⓐ Ⓑ Ⓒ Ⓓ | 41. | Ⓐ Ⓑ Ⓒ Ⓓ | 71. | Ⓐ Ⓑ Ⓒ Ⓓ |
| 12. | Ⓐ Ⓑ Ⓒ Ⓓ | 42. | Ⓐ Ⓑ Ⓒ Ⓓ | 72. | Ⓐ Ⓑ Ⓒ Ⓓ |
| 13. | Ⓐ Ⓑ Ⓒ Ⓓ | 43. | Ⓐ Ⓑ Ⓒ Ⓓ | 73. | Ⓐ Ⓑ Ⓒ Ⓓ |
| 14. | Ⓐ Ⓑ Ⓒ Ⓓ | 44. | Ⓐ Ⓑ Ⓒ Ⓓ | 74. | Ⓐ Ⓑ Ⓒ Ⓓ |
| 15. | Ⓐ Ⓑ Ⓒ Ⓓ | 45. | Ⓐ Ⓑ Ⓒ Ⓓ | 75. | Ⓐ Ⓑ Ⓒ Ⓓ |
| 16. | Ⓐ Ⓑ Ⓒ Ⓓ | 46. | Ⓐ Ⓑ Ⓒ Ⓓ | 76. | Ⓐ Ⓑ Ⓒ Ⓓ |
| 17 | Ⓐ Ⓑ Ⓒ Ⓓ | 47. | Ⓐ Ⓑ Ⓒ Ⓓ | 77. | Ⓐ Ⓑ Ⓒ Ⓓ |
| 18. | Ⓐ Ⓑ Ⓒ Ⓓ | 48. | Ⓐ Ⓑ Ⓒ Ⓓ | 78. | Ⓐ Ⓑ Ⓒ Ⓓ |
| 19. | Ⓐ Ⓑ Ⓒ Ⓓ | 49. | Ⓐ Ⓑ Ⓒ Ⓓ | 79. | Ⓐ Ⓑ Ⓒ Ⓓ |
| 20. | Ⓐ Ⓑ Ⓒ Ⓓ | 50. | Ⓐ Ⓑ Ⓒ Ⓓ | 80. | Ⓐ Ⓑ Ⓒ Ⓓ |
| 21. | Ⓐ Ⓑ Ⓒ Ⓓ | 51. | Ⓐ Ⓑ Ⓒ Ⓓ | | |
| 22. | Ⓐ Ⓑ Ⓒ Ⓓ | 52. | Ⓐ Ⓑ Ⓒ Ⓓ | | |
| 23. | Ⓐ Ⓑ Ⓒ Ⓓ | 53. | Ⓐ Ⓑ Ⓒ Ⓓ | | |
| 24. | Ⓐ Ⓑ Ⓒ Ⓓ | 54. | Ⓐ Ⓑ Ⓒ Ⓓ | | |
| 25. | Ⓐ Ⓑ Ⓒ Ⓓ | 55. | Ⓐ Ⓑ Ⓒ Ⓓ | | |
| 26. | Ⓐ Ⓑ Ⓒ Ⓓ | 56. | Ⓐ Ⓑ Ⓒ Ⓓ | | |
| 27. | Ⓐ Ⓑ Ⓒ Ⓓ | 57. | Ⓐ Ⓑ Ⓒ Ⓓ | | |
| 28. | Ⓐ Ⓑ Ⓒ Ⓓ | 58. | Ⓐ Ⓑ Ⓒ Ⓓ | | |
| 29. | Ⓐ Ⓑ Ⓒ Ⓓ | 59. | Ⓐ Ⓑ Ⓒ Ⓓ | | |
| 30. | Ⓐ Ⓑ Ⓒ Ⓓ | 60. | Ⓐ Ⓑ Ⓒ Ⓓ | | |

Name: _____          Date: _____

STATE PORTION

| | | | | | | | | | |
|---|---|---|---|---|---|---|---|---|---|
| 1. | Ⓐ | Ⓑ | Ⓒ | Ⓓ | 31. | Ⓐ | Ⓑ | Ⓒ | Ⓓ |
| 2. | Ⓐ | Ⓑ | Ⓒ | Ⓓ | 32. | Ⓐ | Ⓑ | Ⓒ | Ⓓ |
| 3. | Ⓐ | Ⓑ | Ⓒ | Ⓓ | 33. | Ⓐ | Ⓑ | Ⓒ | Ⓓ |
| 4. | Ⓐ | Ⓑ | Ⓒ | Ⓓ | 34. | Ⓐ | Ⓑ | Ⓒ | Ⓓ |
| 5. | Ⓐ | Ⓑ | Ⓒ | Ⓓ | 35. | Ⓐ | Ⓑ | Ⓒ | Ⓓ |
| 6. | Ⓐ | Ⓑ | Ⓒ | Ⓓ | | | | | |
| 7. | Ⓐ | Ⓑ | Ⓒ | Ⓓ | | | | | |
| 8. | Ⓐ | Ⓑ | Ⓒ | Ⓓ | | | | | |
| 9. | Ⓐ | Ⓑ | Ⓒ | Ⓓ | | | | | |
| 10. | Ⓐ | Ⓑ | Ⓒ | Ⓓ | | | | | |
| 11. | Ⓐ | Ⓑ | Ⓒ | Ⓓ | | | | | |
| 12. | Ⓐ | Ⓑ | Ⓒ | Ⓓ | | | | | |
| 13. | Ⓐ | Ⓑ | Ⓒ | Ⓓ | | | | | |
| 14. | Ⓐ | Ⓑ | Ⓒ | Ⓓ | | | | | |
| 15. | Ⓐ | Ⓑ | Ⓒ | Ⓓ | | | | | |
| 16. | Ⓐ | Ⓑ | Ⓒ | Ⓓ | | | | | |
| 17 | Ⓐ | Ⓑ | Ⓒ | Ⓓ | | | | | |
| 18. | Ⓐ | Ⓑ | Ⓒ | Ⓓ | | | | | |
| 19. | Ⓐ | Ⓑ | Ⓒ | Ⓓ | | | | | |
| 20. | Ⓐ | Ⓑ | Ⓒ | Ⓓ | | | | | |
| 21. | Ⓐ | Ⓑ | Ⓒ | Ⓓ | | | | | |
| 22. | Ⓐ | Ⓑ | Ⓒ | Ⓓ | | | | | |
| 23. | Ⓐ | Ⓑ | Ⓒ | Ⓓ | | | | | |
| 24. | Ⓐ | Ⓑ | Ⓒ | Ⓓ | | | | | |
| 25. | Ⓐ | Ⓑ | Ⓒ | Ⓓ | | | | | |
| 26. | Ⓐ | Ⓑ | Ⓒ | Ⓓ | | | | | |
| 27. | Ⓐ | Ⓑ | Ⓒ | Ⓓ | | | | | |
| 28. | Ⓐ | Ⓑ | Ⓒ | Ⓓ | | | | | |
| 29. | Ⓐ | Ⓑ | Ⓒ | Ⓓ | | | | | |
| 30. | Ⓐ | Ⓑ | Ⓒ | Ⓓ | | | | | |

## National Portion

1. Which of the following is considered commercial real estate?

   A. Office building
   B. Warehouse
   C. Multifamily house
   D. All of the above

2. Jack is trying to convince Mary to move to a particular neighborhood because the residents there are of her ethnic background and religion. What is guilty of?

   A. Blockbusting
   B. Discriminating
   C. Convincing
   D. Steering

3. What type of lease would a tenant take when using a warehouse for the purpose of manufacturing and distribution?

   A. Gross lease
   B. Net lease
   C. Percentage lease
   D. Proprietary lease

4. What is a notice given on a pending lawsuit?

   A. Lis Pendens
   B. Statute of limitations
   C. Notice of intent
   D. Notice of default

5. Who issues variances?

   A. Architectural Review Board
   B. EPA
   C. Municipal Engineers
   D. Zoning Board of Appeals

6. What is the name given to an individual who originates, sells and services mortgage loans?

   A. Mortgage Banker
   B. Mortgage Broker
   C. Lender
   D. Borrower

7. What is the exterior layer of a house?

   A. Eaves
   B. Flashing
   C. Pitch
   D. Sheathing

8. Who holds on to the security deposit?

   A. Agent
   B. Broker
   C. Buyer
   D. Landlord

9.  What is the term used to define the estimated age of a property based on its utilities and physical wear and tear?

    A.  Economic life
    B.  Effective age
    C.  Use discount
    D.  Depreciation

10. How long are brokers required to hold on to property files?

    A.  One year
    B.  Three years
    C.  Five years
    D.  Never

11. What is the unit used to measure furnace or air conditioner capacity?

    A.  British Thermal Unit
    B.  Bytes
    C.  Joules
    D.  Watts

12. What describes the type of estate granted within a lease?

    A.  Acceleration clause
    B.  Annuity law
    C.  Cancellation clause
    D.  Habendum clause

13. What type of income is income generated from a rental property?

    A.  Active
    B.  Passive
    C.  Portfolio
    D.  All the above

14. What is another name used to refer to land lease?

    A.  Ground lease
    B.  Home lease
    C.  Percentage lease
    D.  Estate lease

15. Which regulations govern the construction details of buildings with the sole interest of safeguarding the occupants and general public?

    A.  APR
    B.  Building codes
    C.  Leasing laws
    D.  Zoning codes

16. If a seller nets $325,000 from the sale of her home, and the commission is 3%, how much did the home sell for?

    A.  $334,750
    B.  $335,051
    C.  $315,250
    D.  $334,027

17. Personal property that is attached to real property, such as a chandelier, is regarded as

A. An emblement
B. An appliance
C. A fixture
D. A liability

18. What are outside amenities that maximize use of property called?

A. Cosmetic improvements
B. Essential improvements
C. Offsite improvements
D. Supplemental improvements

19. Which form of ownership passes the shares of ownership upon death?

A. Life estate
B. Severalty
C. Tenancy in common
D. Joint tenancy

20. If a property manager is fixing a leaky pipe, what type of maintenance is he doing?

A. Aesthetic maintenance
B. Appreciation
C. Breakdown prevention
D. Preventive maintenance

21. Which act was enacted in order to identify hazardous sites?

A. Americans with disabilities Act
B. CERCLA
C. Fair Housing Act
D. Civil Rights Act

22. What is tenancy in common?

A. A shared tenancy in which each holder has a distinct, separately transferable interest
B. A tenancy in which each holder has equal interest, where interest is automatically passed in case of death
C. A tenancy in which interest is returned to the public upon death
D. A tenancy in which a single owner owns full ownership of a property

23. What is the money available after deducting all expenses?

A. Cash out returns
B. Cash flow
C. Cash on cash return
D. Revenue

24. What is an involuntary lien?

A. A lien that arises without the property owner's consent
B. A lien that is initiated with owner's consent
C. A lien that cannot be cashed on
D. None of the above

25. What is the name given to property that legally qualifies as owner's principal property?

    A. Commercial property
    B. Homestead property
    C. Real property
    D. Personal property

26. A person authorized to handle a principal's affairs in one specific area is referred to as?

    A. General agent
    B. Dual agent
    C. Multi agent
    D. Special agent

27. What are real property rights conferred with ownership?

    A. Bundle of rights
    B. Right of first refusal
    C. Riparian rights
    D. Doctrine of equitable conversion

28. What is the fine placed for a violation of license law?

    A. $1,000
    B. $5,000
    C. $6,000
    D. $10,000

29. What is the term for commercial property depreciation?

    A. 5 years
    B. 29 years
    C. 39 years
    D. 40 years

30. The division of expenses at the time of closing between the buyer and seller in proportion to the actual use of a property is called?

    A. Bill of sale
    B. Loan to value ratio
    C. Proration
    D. Tax abatement

31. What is the equivalent of 1 cubic foot?

    A. 5.25 gallons
    B. 7.26 gallons
    C. 7.48 gallons
    D. 10 gallons

32. What is a statement that shows total revenues generated based on rent rolls and management styles?

    A. Invoice statement
    B. Income statement
    C. Pro forma statement
    D. Operating statement

**33.** What type of building is divided into two condominiums where the first is the co-op residential units (80%) and the second is for professional/commercial units (20%)?

  A. Condo
  B. Condop
  C. Co-op
  D. Multi family home

**34.** A person authorized to handle a principal's affairs in more than one specific area is referred to as?

  A. Special agent
  B. General Agent
  C. Dual agent
  D. Broker

**35.** What are the laws that limit the maximum interest rate that can be charged?

  A. APR
  B. Annuity laws
  C. FHA
  D. Usury

**36.** What is the nature of the title in co-op ownership?

  A. Freehold
  B. Leasehold
  C. Regular hold
  D. Lease assignment

**37.** What is a non-possessory interest in property giving a lienholder the right to foreclose?

  A. Mortgage
  B. Duties
  C. Taxes
  D. Revenue

**38.** What is the agreement that allows the tenant to continue living on a property once the lease has expired?

  A. Tenancy in common
  B. Tenancy in entirety
  C. Tenancy in sufferance
  D. Ownership in severalty

**39.** Can a salesperson hold other jobs?

  A. Yes
  B. No
  C. Only if it is in real estate
  D. Maybe

**40.** What does the Secondary Mortgage Market refer to in the loan process?

  A. Buyers that buy houses on mortgage
  B. Sellers that offer buy down arrangement
  C. Lending market
  D. Private investors and government agencies that buy and sell real estate mortgages

**41.** What are air rights?

    A.   Right to breath
    B.   Right to own an airspace
    C.   Right to package air
    D.   Rights granted to a property owner on the vertical space above the property

**42.** What is the relationship where agents work together in the best interest of their respective clients?

    A.   Dual agency
    B.   Single agency
    C.   Co-broking
    D.   Co-borrowing

**43.** What is the legal term for passing responsibility of your apartment onto another tenant?

    A.   Sub lease
    B.   Lease assignment
    C.   Leasehold
    D.   Lease break

**44.** If you have a loan of $200,000 with a 12% interest, how much do you pay in interest every month?

    A.   $1,200
    B.   $2,000
    C.   $2,400
    D.   $24,000

**45.** What are the extra charges above the selling costs that are incurred by the buyer on the purchase of a home?

    A.   Common costs
    B.   Closing costs
    C.   Down payment
    D.   Short fall

**46.** What are the monthly charges imposed on condo tenants?

    A.   Common charges
    B.   Common costs
    C.   Service fees
    D.   Short fall

**47.** What is the name given to the ratio defined by dividing monthly debt payments to gross monthly income?

    A.   Loan to value ratio
    B.   Debt to income ratio
    C.   Earnest money deposit
    D.   Foreclosure

**48.** What is the percentage amount of the selling price that is deposited by the buyer when closing a real estate transaction?

    A.   Down payment
    B.   Escrow
    C.   Earnest money deposit
    D.   Tax abatement

**49.** What is earnest money deposit?

    A. Money deposited by the buyer to the seller to show interest in the purchase of a home
    B. Purchase money
    C. Down payment
    D. Security deposit

**50.** What is the financial agreement that allows a third party to regulate payment where two parties are involved?

    A. Security deposit
    B. Sales deposit
    C. Escrow
    D. Earnest money deposit

**51.** What is the notice given when a tenant is in violation of the lease agreement and is up for eviction?

    A. Notice to cure
    B. Notice of intention
    C. Notice of termination
    D. Notice to quit

**52.** What is the notice given when a squatter is accommodated without the landlord's consent?

    A. Notice of default
    B. Notice of intention
    C. Notice to cure
    D. Notice to quit

**53.** What is the notice given to state that no work has been performed?

    A. Notice of cessation
    B. Notice given to evict an unruly tenant
    C. Notice filed in court by a lender on defaulting of payment
    D. Notice to discontinue the breach of lease within 10 days

**54.** What is the name given to a visit made to a potential property to identify the condition of the house?

    A. Final walk through
    B. Home inspection
    C. Appraisal
    D. Assessment

**55.** What mortgage plan allows a borrower to switch to a fixed-rate mortgage?

    A. Adjustable Rate Mortgage
    B. Convertible ARM
    C. Fixed rate mortgage
    D. Floating rate mortgage

**56.** What is the situation that arises when an individual that is legally required to make payments does not fulfill this obligation?

    A. Delinquency
    B. Defaulting
    C. Escalation clause
    D. Foreclosure

**57.** Which agency insures FHA-approved lenders?

    A.   CERCLA
    B.   Consumer Financial Protection Bureau
    C.   Federal Emergency Management Agency
    D.   Federal Housing Administration

**58.** Which agency is commissioned with overseeing products and services offered to consumers in the finance industry?

    A.   Consumer Financial Protection Bureau
    B.   Federal Housing Administration
    C.   Environmental Protection Agency
    D.   Federal Emergency Management Agency

**59.** What service allows brokers to share their listings?

    A.   Broker Listing Service
    B.   Single Agency Listing
    C.   Multiple Listing Service
    D.   Shared Listing Service

**60.** What is the contract covering household maintenance systems?

    A.   Deed
    B.   Home warranty
    C.   Hazard insurance
    D.   HO4

**61.** What is the name given to a real estate transaction where buyers outbid each other for the property?

    A.   Acceleration clause
    B.   Escalation clause
    C.   Public auction
    D.   Tender

**62.** What is the name given to a notice given showing interest in a property?

    A.   Notice of cessation
    B.   Notice to cure
    C.   Notice of default
    D.   Notice of intent

**63.** What is the increase in the value of a property?

    A.   Appreciation
    B.   Depreciation
    C.   Obsolescence
    D.   All of the above

**64.** What is the mortgage payment plan that involves making payments every fortnight?

    A.   Balloon mortgage
    B.   Biweekly mortgage
    C.   Blanket mortgage
    D.   Graduated mortgage

**65.** What term is used to describe the document attached to an original contract?

   A.   Addendum
   B.   Signed agreement
   C.   Requirements clause
   D.   Terms and conditions

**66.** What refinancing method allows a borrower to acquire cash from the transaction?

   A.   Cash flow
   B.   Cash out refinance
   C.   Cash on cash return
   D.   Refinancing

**67.** Who oversees that code restrictions are followed and construction / renovation are done by licensed professionals?

   A.   Contractor
   B.   Department of Buildings
   C.   Zoning board
   D.   Architectural Review Board

**68.** What is the final stage of a real estate transaction?

   A.   Closing
   B.   Sale
   C.   Final walk through
   D.   Handing of the title

**69.** What is the percentage of the selling price that is usually earned by a real estate agent for facilitating the transaction?

   A.   Bonus
   B.   Commission
   C.   Salary
   D.   Rent

**70.** What is the name of fees paid to the lender at closing in exchange for a reduced interest rate?

   A.   Mortgage
   B.   Service fee
   C.   Discount points
   D.   Principal fee

**71.** Which Act was passed to protect against discrimination in borrowing?

   A.   Equal Credit Opportunity Act
   B.   Fair and Accurate Credit Transaction Act of 2003
   C.   The Fair Credit Reporting Act
   D.   Truth in Lending Act

**72.** What does the phrase "For Sale by Owner" mean?

   A.   A sale is being facilitated by an agent
   B.   Investors are open to receiving offers
   C.   A property sale is being handled without a real estate agent
   D.   All of the above

**73.** What is the name of the document used to summarize all the fees incurred by the lender and borrower during settlement of a loan?

A. Financial statement
B. Invoice
C. IOU
D. Settlement statement

**74.** Which entity determines the assessed value of a property?

A. Building Inspector
B. Municipal council
C. Real estate agent
D. Tax assessor

**75.** If a property is taxed at 40% with a tax levy of $88,000, what is its assessed value?

A. $220,000
B. $146,666
C. $123,200
D. None of the above

**76.** Which type of estate has rights to the property for an indefinite duration?

A. List estate
B. Estate for years
C. Freehold estate
D. Less-than-freehold estate

**77.** Which of the following is **not** an essential element of a deed?

A. Signature of the grantee
B. Date
C. Identification of the grantor and grantee
D. Adequate description of the property

**78.** What is a lessor?

A. A person who leases real estate property from the owner of said property
B. A person that makes a grant
C. The owner of real estate who leases the property to another
D. The person who transfers property by sale

**79.** What is the definition of a joint tenancy?

A. When property is held by two or more parties
B. When a third-party trust owns the property
C. When the seller and the buyer both own the property
D. When the property is inherited by a family member

**80.** What is the definition of a trust deed?

A. The owner of the real estate property who leases the property to another
B. A deed with limited or no warranties
C. A deed that transfers property to a family member
D. A document used when one party has taken out a loan from another party to purchase property

**THIS IS THE END OF THE NATIONAL PORTION.**

## State Portion

1.  Which law protects persons with a disability by prohibiting owners or persons engaging in real estate transactions from engaging in discriminatory practices?

    A.  Michigan Uniform State Antitrust Act
    B.  Michigan Persons with Disabilities Civil Rights Act
    C.  Michigan Disabilities Act
    D.  No such law exists

2.  A(n) _____ states that if the property has been used as a principal residence for 2 of the past 5 years, a person can exclude a specified amount of gain.

    A.  Homestead act
    B.  Capital gain exclusion
    C.  Universal exclusion
    D.  None of the above

3.  This federal act regulates and standardizes real estate procedures and lending practices.

    A.  Real Estate Settlement Procedures Act
    B.  Federal Real Estate Law
    C.  Real Estate Law
    D.  Settlement Act

4.  What is the main reason for the Truth in Lending (Regulation Z) Act?

    A.  To protect the borrower from high interest rates
    B.  To allow the borrower to comparison shop without worrying about hidden costs
    C.  To provide loans for veterans
    D.  None of the above

**5.** In Michigan, the maximum allowable interest on seller financing is _____.

    A.  10%
    B.  11%
    C.  12%
    D.  13%

**6.** The Michigan Uniform State Antitrust Act makes all of the below illegal except _____.

    A.  Dual agency
    B.  Setting commission rates
    C.  Territorial or customer allocation
    D.  Tying services in real estate to another arrangement

**7.** Michigan allows a mortgage broker to be provided a referral fee of up to _____.

    A.  $500
    B.  A referral is not legal in Michigan
    C.  $1,000
    D.  There is no limit on the referral fee

**8.** One of the requirements of this federal act is that a reason for denial must be given to the borrower within 30 days.

    A.  Credit Transparency Act
    B.  Fair Credit Act
    C.  Equal Credit Opportunity Act
    D.  Equality Act

9. The whole state of Michigan is laid out on a grid of _____.

   A. Sections
   B. Survey townships
   C. Meridian lines
   D. Quarter sections

10. The _____ provides the basis for cities and counties to develop long-range plans for growth.

   A. Michigan Survey Act
   B. Federal Zoning Act
   C. Michigan Zoning Enabling Act
   D. None of the above

11. Which law states that once a parcel is split, it cannot be split again for ten years?

   A. Michigan Zoning Act
   B. The Parcel Act
   C. Enabling Act
   D. Michigan Land Division Act

12. What is the purpose of the Michigan Right to Farm Act?

   A. Policy to resolve disputes regarding an actionable nuisance that arise between farms and neighboring residents
   B. Policy protecting farmers from defaulting on loans
   C. Provide equipment and education on farming practices to new farmers
   D. None of the above

**13.** A(n) _____ is a type of leasehold estate in which a tenant stays in possession of a property after the lease has expired.

    A. Tenancy by the entirety
    B. Estate at sufferance
    C. Lifelong tenancy
    D. None of the above

**14.** A(n) _____ occurs where a particular land use is totally excluded from the municipality.

    A. Accepted zoning
    B. Zoning laws
    C. Exclusionary zoning
    D. Municipality zoning

**15.** This type of listing agreement promises the broker a commission if s/he finds the buyer but allows the owner to find a buyer without paying a commission to the buyer.

    A. Sale by owner
    B. Non-exclusive agency listing
    C. Multi-agency listing
    D. Exclusive agency listing

**16.** Depreciation due to an environmental factor is called a(n) _____.

    A. Functional obsolescence
    B. Physical obsolescence
    C. External obsolescence
    D. Aesthetic obsolescence

17. This law is an expansion to the Fair Housing Act and includes families with children and those with physical or mental disabilities.

    A. Fair Housing Amendment Act
    B. Disabilities and Children Act
    C. Additional Fair Housing Act
    D. No such law exists

18. _____ is government sponsored and provides mortgage loans in the secondary mortgage market.

    A. Sallie Mae
    B. Fannie Mae
    C. Veterans Affairs
    D. Housing and Urban Development

19. This is the maximum possible right of ownership of real property.

    A. Fee simple
    B. Fee simple absolute
    C. Absolute ownership
    D. Fee simple defeasible

20. What does a fiduciary relationship mean?

    A. An agreement between a broker and a brokerage
    B. A relationship between a trustee and beneficiary
    C. The agreement to pay a commission
    D. None of the above

21. Michigan practices _____ which means the buyer holds the deed of the property during the mortgage term.

    A. Lien theory
    B. Title theory
    C. Deed ownership
    D. Property ownership

22. This gives a borrower the right to redeem property before a foreclosure sale.

    A. Borrower's rights
    B. Equitable redemption
    C. Redemption right
    D. None of the above

23. A(n) _____ is also referred to as a due on sale clause.

    A. Abandonment clause
    B. Reversal clause
    C. Alienation clause
    D. Acceleration clause

24. A(n) is when a borrower sells their home for less than what they owe the lender.

    A. Collateral
    B. Hardship sale
    C. Quick sale
    D. Short sale

25. In this type of mortgage, the lender provides the homeowner with monthly payments and the homeowner repays the lender with a lump sum at a later time.

    A. Open-end mortgage
    B. Open mortgage
    C. Reverse mortgage
    D. Budget mortgage

26. A _____ is a tax that has been made up of taxes levied on the real estate by government agencies.

    A. Estate tax
    B. General real estate tax
    C. General property tax
    D. No such tax exists

27. This is an estimate of all closing fees that must be provided to a borrower within 3 days of the loan application.

    A. General warranty deed
    B. Good and marketable title estimate
    C. Good faith estimate
    D. Ginne Mae

28. These words state the grantor's intention to convey the property at the present time.

    A. Deed clause
    B. Granting clause
    C. Conveyance clause
    D. Intention clause

29. Water that exists under the earth's surface is called _____.

   A. Groundwater
   B. Riparian
   C. Littoral
   D. Geological formations

30. In this type of loan, the monthly payments increase annually.

   A. Reverse mortgage
   B. Growing-equity mortgage
   C. Term mortgage
   D. Equity mortgage

31. A(n) _____ is the part of the deed that begins with "to have and to hold."

   A. Habendum clause
   B. Acceleration clause
   C. Alienation clause
   D. Granting clause

32. In a _____ the lessee retains possession of the leased property after the lease has expired.

   A. Joint tenancy
   B. Tenancy by the entirety
   C. Holdover tenancy
   D. None of the above

**33.** When a property owner dies without a will, the property passes by what is called _____.

   A. Acknowledgement
   B. Intestate succession
   C. Accrued succession
   D. Beneficiary

**34.** _____ is the illegal practice of inducing a change in the neighborhood for profit by urging residents to sell their homes quickly and at deflated prices.

   A. Bona fide
   B. Arbitration
   C. Commingling
   D. Blockbusting

**35.** An official approval issued by the local government that gives a person permission to proceed with a construction is called a(n) _____.

   A. Zoning permit
   B. Building permit
   C. Construction permit
   D. None of the above

**THIS IS THE END OF THE STATE PORTION.**

# Answer Key – National Portion

| | | | | | | | |
|---|---|---|---|---|---|---|---|
| 1. | D | 21. | B | 41. | D | 61. | B |
| 2. | D | 22. | A | 42. | C | 62. | D |
| 3. | B | 23. | B | 43. | B | 63. | A |
| 4. | A | 24. | A | 44. | B | 64. | B |
| 5. | D | 25. | B | 45. | B | 65. | A |
| 6. | A | 26. | D | 46. | A | 66. | B |
| 7. | D | 27. | A | 47. | B | 67. | B |
| 8. | D | 28. | A | 48. | A | 68. | A |
| 9. | B | 29. | C | 49. | A | 69. | B |
| 10. | B | 30. | C | 50. | C | 70. | C |
| 11. | A | 31. | C | 51. | C | 71. | A |
| 12. | D | 32. | D | 52. | D | 72. | C |
| 13. | B | 33. | B | 53. | A | 73. | D |
| 14. | A | 34. | B | 54. | B | 74. | D |
| 15. | B | 35. | D | 55. | B | 75. | A |
| 16. | B | 36. | B | 56. | A | 76. | C |
| 17. | C | 37. | A | 57. | D | 77. | A |
| 18. | C | 38. | C | 58. | A | 78. | C |
| 19. | D | 39. | A | 59. | C | 79. | A |
| 20. | D | 40. | D | 60. | B | 80. | D |

1.    **D) All of the above**

Commercial property includes mixed use buildings (e.g. retail store on the first floor, residences above) office buildings, hotels, retail stores, multifamily houses, industrial warehouses, and more.

2.    **D) Steering**

Steering is the act of guiding prospective buyers to specified settlement areas based on race, religion and other discriminatory factors.

3.    **B) Net lease**

This is a lease where the tenant pays rent and part of utilities fee and property taxes. The landlord is tasked with paying the utility bills and property taxes that are not covered by the tenant. This lease is common in commercial real estate.

4.     **A) Lis Pendens**

This is a legal notice that a lawsuit concerning a real estate property is pending. Usually involves a property title or claims of ownership interest. Details of a property whose title is in question are required to be filed at the county record to notify future buyers and lenders.

5.     **D) Zoning Board of Appeals**

The Zoning Board of Appeals is a board of select members that is given jurisdiction to hear and decide on appeals regarding zoning laws.

6.     **A) Mortgage Banker**

A mortgage banker is an individual who originates, closes and funds with his own funds or that of a company. Once a mortgage is originated it is either retained or sold to an investor. A mortgage banker has the power to approve or reject a mortgage and earns fees on the origination of a loan.

7.     **D) Sheathing**

Sheathing is a covering structure and acts as a case for the exterior of the home. Usually used to describe a boarding material that forms the roof, floor and walls. It provides a surface for other materials and strengthens weather resistance.

8.     **D) Landlord**

A security deposit is an amount equaling monthly rent that is paid to ensure rent will be paid and to cater for other responsibilities highlighted in the lease. Can also be used as security for unpaid rent and damages and is held onto by the landlord.

9.     **B) Effective age**

This is an estimate of a building age based on its utilities and the wear and tear. It could be the actual age or a little more or less than the actual age. This is dependent on maintenance, remodeling and removal of inadequacies. It is used to determine the remaining life of a building.

10.     **B) Three years**

Brokers are required by law to hold on to a copy of property files for a minimum of 3 years. This is to act as a proof in case of a dispute in the future. These include copies of all listings, deposit receipts, cancelled checks and trust records executed or obtained during the transaction.

Practice Tes

11. **A) British Thermal Unit**

Defined as the amount of heat required to raise the temperature of one pound of water by one-degree Fahrenheit. In the case of air conditioning, it is defined as the number of BTU per hour products that can be added or removed from the air.

12. **D) Habendum clause**

This is a legal agreement that involves the rights and interests of a property being transferred to a lessee. For a leased property there is a transfer of ownership and restrictions on the property. A purchased property is void of restrictions and only transfers ownership.

13. **B) Passive**

This is an income source that requires little to no daily input in order to yield returns.

14. **A) Ground lease**

This is a lease agreement where a tenant is allowed to develop a parcel of land during the lease period. On expiry of the lease, all improvements remain in the owner's custody. Land leases are often last between 50-99 with other agreement allowing for renewal.

15. **B) Building codes**

These are a set of regulations that are put in place to ensure design, construction, alteration and maintenance of structures is done according to the state's requirements. They aim at safeguarding the health, safety and welfare of the occupants.

16. **B) $335,051**

$325,000 / (1 - 0.03) = $335,051

17. **C) A fixture**

A fixture is any physical property that is permanently attached to real property (usually land). Fixtures are treated as a part of real property. Examples of fixtures are ceiling fans and TV mounts.

18. **C) Offsite improvements**

Offsite improvements are amenities that are not within the premise of the structure but are necessary to maximize the use of the property and ultimately increase the value of the property.

19.    **D) Joint tenancy**

Joint tenancy is a form of ownership in which several people own a property together, each with equal shares and rights. If one of the owners in a joint tenancy dies, that owner's share in the property is automatically passed to the remaining owners.

20.    **D) Preventive maintenance**

In order to maintain tenants and an acceptable return on an investment, routine checks and repairs have to be done. These are done to safeguard against failing which may incur losses to the property manager that arise due to cost of replacement.

21.    **B) CERCLA**

The Comprehensive Environmental Response Compensation and Liability Act of 1980 was enacted in order to identify, investigate and facilitate cleanup of hazardous sites. The act is currently administered by the Environmental Protection Agency.

22.    **A) A shared tenancy in which each holder has a distinct, separately transferable interest**

This type of ownership is characterized by ownership between two or more people who can have either equal or unequal shares. Unlike a joint tenancy, if an owner dies, the person's share is passed to his/her heirs and not distributed to the remaining owners.

23.    **B) Cash flow**

This is the amount of profit retained after paying off all operating costs and repurposing amounts made in dividends for use in future repairs. To be able to profit from an investment, one must maintain a positive cash flow.

24.    **A) A lien that arises without the property owner's consent**

Involuntary liens are placed by government facilities for unpaid taxes.

25.    **B) Homestead property**

Homestead laws are laws that exist to ensure to protect owners from losing their home equity while filing for bankruptcy. Homestead property enables an individual to declare a portion of property as homestead to avoid forced sale.

26.    **D) Special agent**

This is an agent engaged to perform a specific duty for a client. Their authority is limited to that particular task that translates in the expiry of the contract once the task is completed.

27. **A) Bundle of rights**

These are legal rights that are granted to a property buyer which include right to possession, control, exclusion, enjoyment and disposition. A property owner is automatically granted the bundle of rights. In a commercial property, different rights can be assigned to different parties.

28. **A) $1,000**

Violation of license laws may result in suspension of a license or a fine of not more than $1,000 paid to the Department of State. A reprimand is given together with the fine.

29. **C) 39 years**

After 39 years a commercial property is eligible for applying for value loss by depreciation in order to reduce property taxes levied

30. **C) Proration**

Proration occurs during corporate action to ensure all shareholders are treated fairly and a company does not deviate from its original target. Shareholders are offered equity or cash and required to elect one. Once the election is done, shareholders are compensated and if the shares or cash are not enough to satisfy the election each shareholder gets their due in both equity and cash.

31. **C) 7.48 gallons**

32. **D) Operating statement**

An operating statement is a financial statement that is done monthly and annually to document the expenses incurred and revenue gained. From the statement one can calculate the net profit or loss within the period.

33. **B) Condop**

This is a real estate building where the housing units are divided into co-op residential units and condos. They offer more flexible rules than a co-op. Condo units are retained or sold separately by the developer.

34. **B) General Agent**

This is an agent that is mandated to represent the principal in more than one affair.

35.  **D) Usury**

These are laws that are laws set in place to protect borrowers from abusive lending such as imposing unusually high interest rates. Lenders usually target with little knowledge on the traditional loan system. An APR is usually set to protect buyers from being exploited by lenders.

36.  **B) Leasehold**

This is a title on a property being leased and scheduled payments are made throughout the term of the lease. Improvements made within the property are either expensed or capitalized depending on their values.

37.  **A) Mortgage**

A mortgage is a voluntary lien taken out to raise funds to buy a property. The lien is entered willingly and therefore possession of the property remains with the debtor.

38.  **C) Tenancy in sufferance**

In this case, a tenant is granted the privilege to live within the premise before landlord decides to ask the tenant to vacate. Terms of the original lease must be met during this period of time. This type of tenancy can only be terminated by a written notice given not less than 30 days before the tenant is expected to move out.

39.  **A) Yes**

There are no laws restricting a real estate salesperson from working multiple jobs.

40.  **D) Private investors and government agencies that buy and sell real estate mortgages**

This is where home loans and servicing rights are bought within the market. Once a home loan is obtained, it is underwritten, financed and services by a lending facility. A lending facility sells loans to the secondary mortgage market in order to replenish loaning money.

41.  **D) Rights granted to a property owner on the vertical space above the property**

The air space is subject to reasonable use by neighboring buildings and aircrafts. Like with property, air rights can be leased or sold.

42.  **C) Co-broking**

This is a situation where two or more agents that are involved in the same the same transaction agree to work together in order to meet the needs of both parties. In this case, the agents are legally required to act in the best interest of the clients.

43. **B) Lease assignment**

A lease assignment is a legal arrangement where the landlord allows a tenant to assign another tenant to lease the apartment. The tenant is responsible for paying rent and utility fees directly to the landlord. In the case of a lease assignment, the previous tenant is held accountable for defaults in unpaid bills by the assignee.

44. **B) $2,000**

($200,000 * 0.12) / 12 = $2,000

45. **B) Closing costs**

These are the extra costs that are usually incurred by a home buyer on top the agreed upon price. They usually include title insurance, attorney fees and lender fees. These costs are negotiable but commonly paid by buyers.

46. **A) Common charges**

These are the monthly charges that are imposed on condo and condop tenants to cover common charges and amenities. They are usually cover maintenance of shared spaces and operation expenses of a building.

47. **B) Debt to income ratio**

This is a way lenders use to calculate the ability of a borrower to manage the monthly payments required in the settlement plan. Borrowers with a higher ratio have been established to experience struggles in meeting the monthly payments. 43% has been determined to be the highest ratio that can be offered credit.

48. **A) Down payment**

A down payment is an amount paid by the buyer to the seller to secure the property. A down payment is usually paid from the buyer's savings. Contrary to common belief, there is no set percentage of down payment that should be placed on a property

49. **A) Money deposited by the buyer to the seller to show interest in the purchase of a home**

This amount is deposited to give the buyer time to look into the title, sanction an appraisal and conduct an inspection of the property. This money can be returned to the buyer only in the case of a contract breach.

50. **C) Escrow**

This arrangement involves a third party that is neutral to the transaction. Usually used to secure payment in an account that can only be released on meeting of all the terms of the agreement. An escrow account is often used in transactions that involve large amounts of money such as real estate. A listing agent open an account and once the terms are signed upon by both the buyer and the seller, the deal is closed.

51. **C) Notice of termination**

This is a notice given to a tenant to end tenancy stating the reason for termination of tenancy, the date by which the tenant is required to vacate the premise and the legal implication of refusing to move.

52. **D) Notice to quit**

This is a notice given by the landlord regarding someone living in the home as a squatter. The notice usually states that the tenant is required to vacate the property within 10 days and the implications of failing to do so.

53. **A) Notice of cessation**

This is notice given by the contractor by the contractee to state that no work regarding construction has been done for a specified period of time. This notice is given in order to begin mechanical liens compensation.

54. **B) Home inspection**

They are an important part of the real estate transaction as one is able to identify the condition of the property being bought. Inspection of facilities such as plumbing, fixtures and foundation condition comes in handy in determining the value of the property.

55. **B) Convertible ARM**

This is a mortgage plan that allows an individual to benefit from the falling interest rates with the option of switching to a fixed-rate payment plan at a small fee. This switch can be made within the second to fifth year of the mortgage payment period.

56. **A) Delinquency**

This is a situation that arises where a borrower that is legally bound with the responsibility to make necessary payments on a loan or a bond interest foregoes paying the loan. Delinquency usually results in penalties depending on the type of loan and reasons behind failed payments.

57. **D) Federal Housing Administration**

This is United States Agency whose goal is to enable low income individual acquire mortgage loans. The agency approves and insures the lenders. An FHA loan requires a loan down payment and a credit score of at least 580.

58. **A) Consumer Financial Protection Bureau**

This is a regulatory agency that is tasked with the responsibility of overseeing the products and services offered to consumers by financial institutions. In the event of mishandling of a consumer, a complaint is filed to the CFPB for resolution.

59. **C) Multiple Listing Service**

This is a system employed by real estate broker that allows them to view each other's listings. Sharing the database amongst a group of brokers enables brokers to identify buyers for properties they are engaged in.

60. **B) Home warranty**

This is a contract made to ensure the cost of maintaining a household are met. It is put in place as a legal assurance that the property is fit for its intended purpose and meets the expectations of the buyer. It is usually taken to protect against expensive home repairs.

61. **B) Escalation clause**

This is a contract that allows a buyer to set a selling price but any offers higher than the stated price will automatically lead to an increase in the set price. This gives sellers an option to outbid each other and help in making the decision for the sale price.

62. **D) Notice of intent**

This is a non-binding proposal between a buyer and seller of a property to negotiate terms of a real estate transaction. It is usually detailed and lays key points on the weight of the transaction. It is usually used to determine the seriousness of the prospective buyer on the property.

63. **A) Appreciation**

This is the increase in the value of an asset over a period of time. It usually occurs due to increased demand or weakening supply.

64. **B) Biweekly mortgage**

This is a mortgage that requires a principal and interest payment plan every two weeks. It usually has a reduced interest rate throughout the lifespan of the loan.

65.     **A) Addendum**

This is an attached document that is usually included as part of the contract during the preparation. It can act as an informal explanatory attachment or to indicate other requirements of the contract that have not been included in the main attachment.

66.     **B) Cash out refinance**

This is where a homeowner refinances a mortgage for more than its value and withdraws the difference amount as cash. It is only possible to borrowers with a 20% equity on their mortgage.

67.     **B) Department of Buildings**

In order to ensure that building codes are adhered to and construction and renovations are done by professionals, a building permit is required for any building or renovation project. A building permit is a go ahead issued by local government to a contractor to construct or remodel a building. It is issued to ensure that building codes are adhered to and standards are maintained.

68.     **A) Closing**

This is the final stage of a real estate transaction. At this point, the date where contract becomes active is agreed on. On the closing date, the property is legally transferred from the seller to the buyer.

69.     **B) Commission**

This is the percentage earned by a real estate agent for effort placed in facilitating the transaction. It is usually between 5-6% of the sales price and is paid by the seller on closing. It is usually split between the buyer's and seller's agent.

70.     **C) Discount points**

Also referred to as mortgage points, these are fees paid directly to a lender by a homebuyer at closing time. They are usually paid in exchange for lower interest rates reducing monthly payments on the mortgage.

71.     **A) Equal Credit Opportunity Act**

This act was enacted in 1974 and rules it unlawful for lenders to discriminate against loan applicants based on gender, race, age and religion.

72. **C) A property sale is being handled without a real estate agent**

This phrase is used to declare that a property sale is being handled without a real estate agent. While using real estate agents to facilitate sale, some home sellers would rather avoid agents in order to save on the amount spent on commission. In this case the seller must disclose that they are not using an agent.

73. **D) Settlement statement**

This is a document that is usually used to summarize expenses incurred during a loan translation and varies according to loan types. It is usually part of the closing package that must be reviewed and signed by the borrower when closing a loan. A comprehensive settlement statement is legally required for every loan.

74. **D) Tax assessor**

An official whose responsibility is to determine the value of each taxable property in a region.

75. **A) $220,000**

$88,000 / 0.4 = $220,000

76. **C) Freehold estate**

An estate that has exclusive rights of the property for an undefined length of time. The three types of freehold estates are fee simple absolute, fee simple defeasible and life estate.

77. **A) Signature of the grantee**

The grantee does not need to sign a deed. A deed needs to be in writing, must be signed by the grantor, the grantor must have the legal capacity to transfer the property, the grantor and grantee must be identified, the property must be described adequately, the deed must be legally delivered to the grantee and the grantee must accept the deed.

78. **C) The owner of real estate who leases the property to another**

A person who grants a lease to someone else. This person is the owner of the real estate and leases it a lessee through an agreement.

79. **A) When property is held by two or more parties**

It is an agreement in which two or more people own a property with equal rights and obligations. Joint tenancy is typically entered at the same time and through a deed. If one of the owners were to die their portion of the property would automatically pass to the survivors.

80. **D) A document used when one party has taken out a loan from another party to purchase property**

It represents an agreement between the borrower and the lender in which the property is held in a trust managed by a third party until the borrower pays off the loan. The legal title of the property is transferred to the third party to hold. Trust deeds are used in place of mortgages in numerous states.

# Answer Key – State Portion

| | | | |
|---|---|---|---|
| 1. | B | 21. | A |
| 2. | C | 22. | B |
| 3. | A | 23. | C |
| 4. | B | 24. | D |
| 5. | B | 25. | C |
| 6. | A | 26. | B |
| 7. | B | 27. | C |
| 8. | C | 28. | B |
| 9. | B | 29. | A |
| 10. | C | 30. | B |
| 11. | D | 31. | A |
| 12. | A | 32. | C |
| 13. | B | 33. | B |
| 14. | C | 34. | D |
| 15. | D | 35. | B |
| 16. | C | | |
| 17. | A | | |
| 18. | B | | |
| 19. | B | | |
| 20. | B | | |

1. **B) Michigan Persons with Disabilities Civil Rights Act**

   This law protects people with disabilities from discrimination by an owner or anyone who is engaging in a real estate transaction.

2. **C) Universal exclusion**

   This provides an exclusion if the property has been used as a principal residence for at least two of the past five years. It is a $250,000 or a single filing and $500,000 for a joint filing.

3. **A) Real Estate Settlement Procedures Act**

   This law prohibits kickbacks and limits the amount of taxes and insurance to be escrowed. It requires that the lender provide the borrower a good faith estimate of settlement costs and an educational booklet within three days of the application.

4. **B) To allow the borrower to comparison shop without worrying about hidden costs**

   This act requires that a lender uses a uniform measure called the APR. The APR combines the interest rate, loan fee, discount points and other charges for obtaining the loans.

5. **B) 11%**

Usury is charging more interest than the law allows, this is different by each state and there are exceptions. Criminal usury is set at 25%

6. **A) Dual Agency**

Dual agency is an act that is not illegal under the Michigan Uniform Antitrust Act. Others include price fixing, boycotts or conspiring to boycott a competitor or tying agreements.

7. **B) A referral is not legal in Michigan**

Michigan does not allow real estate agents, title companies, mortgage brokers or other to accept referral fees.

8. **C) Equal Credit Opportunity Act**

This federal law requires financial institutions to make credit available to all without regard to race, color, religion, national origin, sex or marital status, age, or receipt of income from public assistance.

9. **B) Survey townships**

A survey township is a square unit of land (36 square miles) and the grid was laid out using GLO and USPLSS.

10. **C) Michigan Zoning Enabling Act**

The planning and zoning in Michigan are based on police power of the government to enable it to protect the health, safety, and welfare of the people.

11. **D) Michigan Land Division Act**

This state law regulates the division of land and promotes the health, safety, and general welfare of the public.

12. **A) Policy to resolve disputes regarding an actionable nuisance that arise between farms and neighboring residents**

This act is a law that resolves disputes between farms and neighboring residents when neighbors or local governments allege that practices on the farm constitute an actionable nuisance.

Practice Tes

13. **B) Estate at sufferance**

This type of tenancy occurs when a lessee lawfully comes into possession of a landlord's real estate but who continues to occupy the premises improperly after his or her lease rights have expired.

14. **C) Exclusionary zoning**

The use of zoning in a manner that excludes it from specific zoning districts persona protected by law from discrimination.

15. **D) Exclusive agency listing**

This type of listing allows the buyer to find a buyer on his/her own without having to pay a commission to the broker.

16. **C) External obsolescence**

This is a factor that reduces the value of a property due to something that is external to the property.

17. **A) Fair Housing Amendment Act**

This expands the Fair Housing Act and includes families with children and those with physical or mental disabilities.

18. **B) Fannie Mae**

This government sponsored organization was established to purchase any kind of mortgage loans in the secondary mortgage market from the primary lenders.

19. **B) Fee simple absolute**

This is land ownership without any limitations or conditions. It is typically created when a deed gives the land with no conditions.

20. **B) A relationship between a trustee and beneficiary**

This is a relationship of trust and confidence. It is between a principal and agent.

21. **A) Lien theory**

When the buyer promises to make all payments to the lender, the mortgage becomes a lien on the property, but the buyer holds the title. The lien is removed one all the payments are made.

22.  **B) Equitable redemption**

This provides the borrower the opportunity to redeem the property before the sale.

23.  **C) Alienation clause**

Most mortgages contain this clause and require the borrower to pay off the debt in full if the property is transferred.

24.  **D) Short sale**

If a borrower is in a hardship situation, they may sell the home for less than what they owe.

25.  **C) Reverse mortgage**

In this type of mortgage, the owner repays the mortgage at a later time as a lump sum and the lender provides the monthly payments.

26.  **B) General real estate tax**

This tax is from taxes that have been levied on the real estate by government agencies and municipalities.

27.  **C) Good faith estimate**

This is required by the Real Estate Settlement Procedures Act and must be provided to the borrower within three days of the loan application.

28.  **B) Granting clause**

These are words that state the grantor's intention to convey the property at the present time in a deed of conveyance. It is generally worded as "convey and warrant", "grant" and "grant, bargain, and sell."

29.  **A) Groundwater**

Water that exists under the earth's surface in the tiny spaces or crevices in geological formations.

30.  **B) Growing-equity mortgage**

In this type of loan, the monthly payments increase annually. The increased amount is used to reduce the principal balance outstanding and thus shorten the overall term of the loan.

31. **A) Habendum clause**

This clause follows the granting clause and defines the extent of ownership the grantor is conveying.

32. **C) Holdover tenancy**

In this type of tenancy, a lessee retains possession of leased property after the lease has expired and the landlord agrees to the tenant's continued occupancy as defined by state law.

33. **B) Intestate succession**

If a property owner dies without leaving a valid will, the title to the property passes to the decedent's heir as provided in the state law of descent.

34. **D) Blockbusting**

This is also called panic peddling and is a violation of the federal civil rights laws. In Michigan this is also illegal with respect to age.

35. **B) Building permit**

This is authorization, in writing, from the local government that allows the construction or remodeling of improvements within its jurisdiction.

# Resources

## 3.1 Finding a broker

Now that you've passed the exam, it's time to officially become an agent! Below is a list of companies and their websites to help you expedite your job search and help you start your journey in selling your first property!

Armada Real Estate Services – https://www.armadarealestate.com/
Best Homes Title Agency – https://besthomestitle.com/
Boji Group – https://www.bojigroup.com/
Cabrio Properties – https://www.cabrioproperties.com/
Capital Title Insurance Agency – https://www.capitaltitle.net/
Ford Land – https://fordland.com/
Fortis Net Lease – https://fortisnetlease.com/
Friedman Real Estate – https://www.friedmanrealestate.com/
Hayman Company – https://www.haymancompany.com/
Keystone Commercial Real Estate – http://www.keystonecres.com/
L. Mason Capitani – https://lmcap.com/
Landmark Commercial Real Estate Services – https://landmarkcres.com/
Locations Commercial Real Estate Services – http://www.locationsmi.com/
MAVD – http://www.mavd.com/
Oxford Companies–https://oxfordcompanies.com/

Pilot Property Group – https://pilotpg.com/
Real Estate One – https://www.realestateone.com/
Signature Associates Commercial Real Estate – https://www.signatureassociates.com/
Stewart Commercial Group – https://svna2.com/
Swisher Commercial – https://swishercommercial.com/

## 3.2 Interviewing

Congratulations! You did get the interview.  Now, just a little work and you can ace it!

First, start by going to all of the social media pages associated with your potential employer.  Focus on several interesting things that they do and specialize in. Look at which type of listings they are showing on their pages and what types of neighborhoods they appear for listings. Look up the particular broker you are interviewing with and go to his/her LinkedIn page and learn more about her/him.

While you're looking at your potential employer's social media pages, take a look at your own. Are there any posts on your Facebook or other social media sites that need to be removed?  Employers are looking at your pages. Anything inappropriate needs to go!

Real estate is all about creating a network of potential clients who trust that what you're selling to them will meet their needs. This means you must understand to differentiate between a client looking to buy a house to raise their newborn and a client who is looking for long term appreciation.

Try simulating cold calls by opening up random properties on Zillow or Trulia, studying them for 2 minutes, and then trying to sell your friend on these properties. They will most likely be asking similar questions to actual prospective buyers or sellers, so it's a very useful exercise in preparing yourself for the mock cold call during the interview.

In addition, study the geography of your broker's city to make sure you don't go in completely blind. Get familiar with the prices and trends in those areas and even take a tour. Drive or walk around and know the neighborhood like the back of your hand so you can impress the employer

On the day of the interview choose your outfit carefully. You should wear some type of suit and make sure your shoes are in good condition. Ask a friend to give you input on the clothes that make you look the most professional. Make sure you brushed your teeth, and your hair is neatly styled. Make sure you don't smell of smoke as most workplaces are smoke-free. No perfume or cologne – your new office may be perfume free. Never chew gum! You will not get the job!

When you arrive at the interview, always make sure to greet the receptionist. Every person you meet at your potential future employer is important!  Make a good impression.

When you land the interview, it's important to have certain answers prepared to more commonly asked questions. First, let's look at general types of questions that you may be asked at any type of interview:

1. Tell me about yourself. This is not the time to talk about everything that happened to you from birth. This is an opportunity to show off a certain drive or characteristic or hobby that is special and helps to explain why you are seeking that particular job. For example, did you participate in a lot of team sports or a lot of clubs in high school or college? Did you work on volunteer projects that required you to meet a lot of new people of all ages and work with them and/or help them? The interviewer has your resume (Always bring extras with you!), so you do not have to spout off all of your previous education and positions. Devote just a sentence or two to that part of your answer.

2. What are your greatest strengths and weaknesses? This is a very tricky question. We all know our strengths; winning personality, gets along with everyone, good at math, good at negotiating, etc., but what about our weaknesses? Well, you certainly want to be honest but now isn't the time to confess all. Choose one. Do you take too long sometimes on a project because you want every detail to be perfect? Do you sometimes want to do something completely by yourself, but you really would be better off asking others for help? These are just two examples of weaknesses that won't sound like you are unprepared for your new job.

3. Where do you see yourself in 5 years? This seems pretty straightforward but be careful. The person interviewing you could be a manager. It is best not to say that you want his/her job. Instead, it may be better to say, I see myself expanding into new roles, doing what I do better, expanding my client base, becoming more successful, continuing my real estate education, and similar phrases.

4. Why did you choose our Company? Everyone asks this question. If you haven't gone to the Company's website, don't go to the interview. You should know everything about the Company and the local office where you are interviewing. You should know which type of real estate they specialize in, how long it's been in business, any recent mergers or expansions, the physical area it is licensed to practice in, and as much as you find on their website and Facebook page and other social media.

5. Why should I hire you and not the next person? This is your moment in the spotlight. Don't just say "pick me!!". Here is a sample: "All of my life, I have enjoyed working with people; when I worked at X company or volunteered at Y organization, I was able to get along with all types of people from children to the elderly. I also have been on teams or worked on teams, and I enjoy it greatly. I like to help people, and there is no bigger purchase than a home. I believe that I have the people skills and the real estate knowledge that I need to be a successful addition to your Company.

6. Why are you leaving your current job? This is not the moment to say how much you dislike your current manager or co-worker. Always be positive at your interview. You can talk about the lack of advancement opportunities, a salary freeze, future layoff being expected, change in your current employer's office location, or some other concrete reason. You can even say that you don't feel all of your skills are being utilized, and you want to use your new knowledge every day in your job.

7. Give me an example of a situation where you used teamwork to accomplish your goal. Even if you only work by yourself at your current job, look back to previous jobs and have the answer

ready. If you don't have a job that matches, think about your volunteer activities at your children's school or at a community center or retirement village.

8. Would you rather work by yourself or as part of a team?  This may be a good one to answer with a bit of vagueness. You can say that it depends on what the assignment might be. Do you have to give a major presentation to a commercial client?  That might be a great time to ask for input and help as needed. Do you have to write a simple analysis of a problem?  Maybe you feel more comfortable completing this on your own. You might want to say that it is very important to ask for feedback from co-workers and managers on projects and on small assignments when you have questions or reach a dead end.

9. What type of manager do you prefer? Do you prefer to work independently or to have more direction? This is always a tricky one as well. Make sure, once again, that you don't diss any of your former managers. A good response would be that you expect some direction from your manager. You feel that you know generally when you need help and would be sure to ask your manager for direction at those times. Also, you welcome all constructive feedback. It is very important to show that you are open to learning and open to change.

10. Why do you have gaps on your resume? Make sure you know the answer in advance to this question. Were you raising a family, taking care of an elderly parent, moving across the country due to a partner relocation, volunteering, etc.? Whatever it is, make sure to answer this one without any hesitation and move on.

11. What is customer service? Be careful with this one. There are two types of customers – internal and external.  Everyone you work with in your office is an internal customer; others are external. The same level of consideration should be given to both internal and external customers. Speak about how important it is to answer questions, do tasks that are needed, go above and beyond the average effort, and ask for help if you don't know the answers.

12. Are you organized? No one wants to admit they are disorganized. If you are going into real estate where there are mounds of paperwork and so many different elements to keep track with, let's assume that every person interviewing for this position must be organized!

13. What do you do when several people give you tasks to do, and it is clear to you that you will not be able to finish them on time?

14. Tell me about a time when you went above and beyond what was required? Hopefully, this will be an easy one to answer. Think about a suggestion you made to your manager to take on more work when a fellow employee was out sick or a time when you thought the presentation needed a special PowerPoint and you produced it.

15. Tell me about a time you had to deal with a difficult person and how you managed to diffuse the situation? You really need to think about this one in advance. If you can't think of a difficult person in your professional life, think about a friend of a friend or someone else. Always acknowledge a difficult person's feelings and avoid arguing about strong opinions that impact an issue that isn't really that important.

Resourc

16. If we offer you the position, how much notice do you have to give to your current employer? Be prepared to know the answer to this one. If you say that you can leave tomorrow, your future employer may not be pleased. It shows that you are not being loyal to your current employer by leaving them in the lurch. Two weeks is standard practice, but if you have a contract, be sure to read it.

Then, you will be asked more specific questions that are relevant to the real estate industry or this particular job. These include but are not limited to:

1. Why do you want to work in the real estate business?
2. This is a commission-based business, which means there is no ceiling to how much you can earn, but it also means there is no floor either. Are you open to this?
3. Let's go through a mock cold call together. I'll be the buyer, and you'll be the seller's agent.
4. How would you sell a property in a neighborhood you've never been to before?
5. A couple is looking to buy their first home. What kind of houses would you suggest?
6. A seasoned investor is looking for investment properties. By coincidence, the Independence Hall is for sale and you are the seller's agent. Pitch it to them.
7. A retiree is looking to sell their house. He is unsure about whether it's a good time to sell it. Explain to them why it is a good time to put the property on the market.

Be prepared to answer technical questions you may have studied for your exam such as:

1. What is the difference between a joint tenancy and a tenancy by the entireties?
2. What is the difference between a cooperative and a condominium?
3. Why is title insurance important?
4. Why would a buyer agree to lease back to a seller?
5. What are the duties of a buyer's agent?
6. What is a tax credit opposed to a tax deduction?
7. What is an easement?
8. Why would someone want to partition property, and what does this mean?
9. When would there be a lien on real estate?
10. What happens at settlement?
11. Why would a homeowner agree to finance a second mortgage for the buyer?

At the end of an interview, the interviewer will always ask if you have any questions. It is never a good idea to say, "No"! Here are some suggestions:

1. If I work here full time, what would be a range of the commissions I could expect in the first year?
2. What type of commission structure is there? Are commissions paid immediately upon closing? What types of fees am I required to pay out-of-pocket? Do I pay any advertising, computer, or other fees?
3. How often would I normally be assigned floor duty? If I answer the phone while on floor duty, do I get that listing?
4. How many open houses would I normally attend a month?
5. What is your hiring process timewise?
6. Do you pay for continuing education?

7. Although I know there isn't a truly "typical" day, what kinds of activities will I be performing during my first few weeks on the job?
8. When I attend my first settlement, will someone more senior come with me to the closing?
9. Will I attend all of the inspections for my listings?
10. What are the types of problems that arise at settlement?
11. Do you give out a list of mortgage brokers to clients?
12. How many people work in this office?
13. Is there coordination with other nearby offices – both this brand and others?
14. Do you provide a list of mortgage brokers to the buyer?

When you are finished with your interview, make sure to thank the interviewer, ask for her/his card, and thank the receptionist before you leave. Every impression counts! When you arrive home, if you really do want to work at that office, within 24 hours write a short email thank you note to your interviewer. If you don't hear back within a week, you can send a brief follow-up e-mail expressing your continuing interest in the position.

Made in United States
Orlando, FL
26 June 2023

34549031R00104